S0-BAD-321

*The Eisenhower presidency
and American foreign policy*

LIBRARY OF POLITICAL STUDIES

GENERAL EDITOR:
PROFESSOR H. VICTOR WISEMAN
Department of Government
University of Exeter

The Eisenhower presidency and American foreign policy

by David B. Capitanchik

Lecturer in Politics
University of Aberdeen

LONDON

ROUTLEDGE & KEGAN PAUL

NEW YORK: HUMANITIES PRESS

First published 1969
by Routledge & Kegan Paul Ltd
Broadway House, 68-74 Carter Lane
London, EC4
Printed in Great Britain by
Northumberland Press Limited, Gateshead
SBN 7100 6641 4

Contents

CONTENTS

General editor's introduction

This series of monographs is designed primarily to meet the needs of students of government, politics, or political science in universities and other institutions providing courses leading to degrees. Each volume aims to provide a brief general introduction indicating the significance of its topic, e.g. executives, parties, pressure groups, etc., and then a longer 'case study' relevant to the general topic. First-year students will thus be introduced to the kind of detailed work on which all generalisations must be based, while more mature students will have an opportunity to become acquainted with recent original research in a variety of fields. The series will eventually provide a comprehensive coverage of most aspects of political science in a more interesting manner than in the large volume which often fails to compensate by breadth what it inevitably lacks in depth.

The study of U.S. politics, perhaps more than that of any other country, needs to combine a general understanding of the main features with more detailed examination of a large number of illustrative examples. This is especially true of the Presidency, which has not only changed more than any other institution since the Founding Fathers, but presents new aspects for study under each one of its incumbents. Organisation and style both reflect the different approaches to and the conception of the office and the role of its incumbent. Further, these distinctive features are perhaps most clearly seen in the conduct of foreign and defence policy. The Eisenhower approach was profoundly different from that of Truman and again from that of Kennedy and Johnson. This case study, therefore, should be a useful addition to the material already available on the most powerful executive office in the world in a field which is of concern not merely to Americans, but to the world as a whole.

H.V.W.

Introduction

A typology, consisting of three major factors, or clusters of factors, has recently been proposed for use in explaining how foreign-policy decisions are arrived at. These are the occasion for decision (or the time and situation), the individual decision-maker, and the organisational context in which he decides (Robinson & Snyder, 1965).

This study is orientated towards the view, articulated by George Modelski, which regards policy-makers as the focus of foreign policy-making. In Modelski's view, for all practical purposes, the policy-making power must be traceable to a limited number of individuals in supreme authority who, because of their supreme authority, are able to determine the overall direction of policy, who can co-ordinate the activities of subordinate agencies and iron out disagreements between them, who can overrule lower-level decisions that are contrary to general policy, and who do, in fact, assume responsibility for what happens, so that they can be blamed for failure and praised for success. Theoretically the policy-maker stands midway between the flow of internal and external influences emanating from the domestic and international environment in which he operates and the decisions that determine the actions of the policy-maker himself towards the outside world. The reader who is familiar with Professor David Easton's analysis of political systems will recognise the similarity between this approach and his.

The basic assumption which underlies this study is that the concept of the 'policy-maker' is crucial for any theoretical analysis of foreign policy-making. A second assumption upon which this study is based, follows from the first. It is that, given centrality of the role of the policy-maker in the foreign policy-making process, the personality, past experience (including profession, occupation, education), the values or attitudes of the policy-maker are significant for the policy-making process and the resulting decisions. In other words, it is assumed, in the case of an individual in supreme authority—in this instance the President of the United States of America—his background and past experience, his conceptions of his role and of the office that he happens to be occupying, together with his outlook generally, are likely to influence at least the way policy is made, if not the actual substance of the policy itself. W. W. Rostow, for example, has pointed out that

It is something of a miracle of American life and bureaucratic structure that the personality and operating style of the President manage somehow to touch and to suffuse the way business comes to be conducted even in the most humble and remote corner of the massive federal enterprise. Washington under Roosevelt, Truman and Eisenhower bore intimately the marks of three distinct and different men (Rostow, 1960, i.387).

None of this is to deny the assumption in the opening paragraph of this Introduction, that foreign policy decisions are the result of the inter-action of situation and individual and organisational factors. That, in other words, the individual, however central, is only one of three major elements in the policy-making process. However, as opposed to the orthodox foreign policy decision-making approach which tends to emphasise the constraints upon the influence of the individual in the process, the emphasis here is on the implications for the process of a particular individual and his personal characteristics.

Clearly, a study of the effect of the individual on the

policy-making process should be broadly comparative in order to be able to answer key questions such as, for example, 'What, if any, policy positions are systematically favoured or disadvantaged by variations in recruitment and socialisation, and what kinds of experience are associated with what kinds of styles of decisional performances?' (Robinson & Snyder, 1965, i. 447). This study, however, is necessarily less ambitious. The aim here is to relate American foreign-policy during a particular period of time to the attitudes and conceptions of a certain individual in supreme authority. In other words, this study uses a scheme of analysis which, it is hoped, might eventually, by providing material for comparison, make it possible to estimate the impact of personality on the policy-making process.

The subject of this study is President Eisenhower and his influence on American foreign policy in the 1950's. Eisenhower has been chosen largely because, in the opinion of most commentators, his influence on the policy-making process was far less than that of other modern Presidents, and that his conception of his office, unique in modern times, had unfortunate consequences for American foreign policy. The Eisenhower Presidency, however, deserves a re-evaluation, if only because it illustrates how the President influences policy, even when his conception of his role precludes that he take a highly active part in the policy-making process.

Schematically, the study falls into four parts. The first three deal with Eisenhower's background and experience, his conceptions of his role and of the office of the Presidency. The fourth chapter considers the implications of these for American foreign policy in the 1950's.

1
Eisenhower's background and experience

The first chapter of this study is necessarily biographical, since it is based on the assumption that the background and experience of an individual in supreme authority—in this case a particular President of the United States—determine, to a considerable extent, the performance of his role.

Eisenhower's early years

Dwight David Eisenhower was unique among the modern Presidents, i.e. those Presidents to have held office since 1933, in that his entire career before his election in 1952, with the exception of the two years he served as President of Columbia University, was spent in uniform. Historically, however, there is nothing unusual in the American experience in a soldier turned President. The thirty-fourth President of the United States, Eisenhower was in fact the tenth general to be elected. More significantly, however, Eisenhower was unique among the modern Presidents in that he had never held elective office in his pre-Presidential career. Nowadays a state governorship or membership of the U.S. Senate is regarded as a *sine qua non* for aspiring Presidential candidates, and five of Eisenhower's military predecessors (Washington, Jackson, Harrison, Pierce and Garfield) had held elective office at some time in their careers before becoming President.

Nevertheless, despite Eisenhower's own statement in his memoirs that before 1952 he was a political novice (Eisenhower, I, 1963), it would be untrue to maintain, as, for example, one writer has done, that he had no real preparation for office (Warren, 1964). The question of what preparation an individual requires to fulfil the office of the Presidency is a highly complex one which merits a study on its own, but there can be little doubt that Eisenhower's experience in the all-important sphere of foreign affairs was uncommon among the modern Presidents. Although it must be admitted that the nature of this experience did leave him, also, with some correspondingly uncommon conceptions of certain aspects of his role as President.

The political journalist Richard Rovere has said that what was known of Eisenhower's career in 1950 consisted of twenty-seven years as an obscure Army officer and eight years as a figure of international repute and importance (Rovere, 1956). However, in discussing Eisenhower's background and experience, some account, however brief, must be taken of his early life. As opposed to the aristocratic background of Franklin D. Roosevelt and the millionaire Boston upbringing of President Kennedy, Eisenhower was the son of an undistinguished family, born literally on the wrong side of the tracks. If his life represents the typical American success story, then this does not seem to have been prompted by any overriding ambition on his part, but rather, as Sidney Warren has put it, because he happened to be in the right place at the right time (Warren, 1964). Very little reliable material is available on Eisenhower's formative years, although Eisenhower himself has recently published a collection of stories (Eisenhower, 1968) comprising his own reminiscences of his early life. All the evidence seems to indicate, that, though poor, Eisenhower had a normal childhood and a secure home background. No doubt this was an important factor in moulding his remarkably uncomplicated personality. As Richard Rovere says, it is a 'standard-American personality . . . forthright, pragmatic, gregarious, alert, calmly energetic, more shrewd than wise, generous, courteous, but neither courtly nor grand, modest but never humble'

(Rovere, 1956, i. 8). Probably the greatest factor in mould-ing Eisenhower's personality was the influence of his mother. An apparently indomitable woman who refused to be broken by financial disaster, according to Sidney Warren, she impressed for all time on her sons that inner despondency or distress must never be exposed to the world. The façade should always be optimistic and cheerful (Warren, 1964). Only those close to Eisenhower felt the effect of his volatile temper. For example, *The New York Times* reported on 4th November 1956 that when Eisen-hower first heard about the Israel invasion and the action of the British and French at the time of Suez, the White House rang with barrack-room language that had not been heard at 1600 Pennsylvania Avenue since the days of General Grant (Finer, 1964). However, while it might have been true that as President his apparent equanimity was at times more a studied pose than an indication of his true state of mind, he rarely showed his temper before reporters, and on other public occasions, at Press conferences in particular, he did not indulge in the criticism, scorn and name-calling that reporters sometimes suffered at the hands of Roosevelt and Truman.

Eisenhower entered the Army the year after he graduated from high school in 1910. He seems not to have had any burning ambition for a military career. He left school un-decided how he would spend his life, but determined, he has recently written (Eisenhower, 1968), to follow his brother Edgar to the University of Michigan. However, while working in a creamery as a labourer, Eisenhower was influenced by a friend to apply for West Point Military Academy. From 1915, when he graduated from West Point, until 1929 Eisenhower was constantly moving about on routine assignments. It has been argued that these years, and for that matter until 1942, when his assignments were somewhat less routine, could not be regarded as years of preparation for high office.

Eisenhower's early years seem very different from those of President Kennedy. In marked contrast to Eisenhower's upbringing, Kennedy was trained for the Presidency virtually from birth. On both sides of his family, for two generations, there was a strong tradition of active participation in politics. President Kennedy's father, Joseph, was a close friend of Franklin Roosevelt, and his vast wealth made it possible for his sons to obtain the best education money could buy. The future President was educated at an expensive New England preparatory school, then studied at Harvard and for a short period at the London School of Economics. Decorated for heroism in the Pacific theatre during the Second World War, he subsequently worked as a political journalist in Britain and Europe. In 1946, at the age of twenty-nine, he was elected to the House of Representatives, with his path undoubtedly eased by his father's wealth and influence.

Much of Eisenhower's early life, far from being years of preparation and ripening for office, was characterised by the boredom suffered by most peacetime officers. His serious reading seems to have consisted principally of military histories. He was particularly interested in the American Civil War, though it is known that during World War II he spent what little leisure he had reading cowboy books.

Pre-war experience

If we regard Eisenhower's early years as being undistinguished, then his meteoric rise to the position of decisive international importance which he occupied during World War II demands explanation. Clearly we need to look more closely at his career, particularly from 1929 onwards. However, we should notice that in 1926 Eisenhower graduated top in a class of 275 officers at the Army's Command and General Staff School at Fort Leavenworth. Moreover, a subsequent assignment in Washington in 1927, when he was given the job of preparing a guide-book to American battlefields in Europe during World War I, brought him together with his younger brother, Milton, who was achieving rapid promotion in government service. Milton was to serve as right-hand man to a number of Republican Secretaries of Agriculture, and then served one of the leading architects of the New Deal, Henry A. Wallace. Already at this time the Eisenhowers had begun to familiarise themselves with civilian Washington. Through his friendship with Harry C. Butcher, a rising young executive of the Columbia Broadcasting System, later to serve as Eisenhower's aide and confidant during World War II, the future President began to establish a reputation of being knowledgeable in public relations, a clever, attractive officer who understood something more than just military drill.

Eisenhower himself has said, perhaps over-modestly, that his military duties prior to the outbreak of World War II gave him at least a fringe familiarity with decisions affecting high officials of the Executive branch (Eisenhower, I, 1963). In 1929, for example, Eisenhower was appointed, as a major, to the post of personal assistant to the Assistant Secretary of War, and subsequently, in February 1933, to the Chief of Staff of the Army, Douglas MacArthur. In his work he was concerned with such matters as military budgets, public relations and relations between the Executive branch and the Congress. There were positive and negative sides both to this experience, and to Eisenhower's subsequent relationship, during Word War II and after, with the Executive and Congress. It was clearly an advantage to have observed something of the top-level decision-making process and personalities at relatively close quarters. On the other hand, his relations with the Congress after he became President was marked by what W. W. Rostow has described as a general dedication to the idea of consensus achieved by accord rather than by political struggle : an attitude reinforced by an Army officer's habit of deference to the legislative branch, which traditionally controlled the Army's purse-strings and much else (Rostow, 1960).

In 1935, MacArthur was appointed military adviser to the Government of the Philippine Islands, and he took Eisenhower with him as his senior assistant. In this capacity

Eisenhower was involved in writing the Commonwealth Defence Act; he helped in the establishment of the Philippine Military Academy, and was in charge of the organisation of the Philippine Air Force. As he reports in his memoirs, his duties brought him into frequent and direct contact with the President of the Commonwealth, as it then was, and presented him with unusually good opportunities to learn about the difficulties in the life of a chief executive (Eisenhower, I, 1963).

Eisenhower returned to the United States in January 1940. Until Pearl Harbour, 7th December 1941, he served first as Chief of Staff of an army division, then of a corps and, finally, from June 1941, of the U.S. Third Army. There can be little doubt that Eisenhower exhibited considerable executive ability in these posts, rising in the course of a year from the rank of colonel, the height of his military ambition, to that of brigadier-general (temporary).

Wartime experience

Had Eisenhower been a conventional general, commanding troops directly in battle, then, no matter how successful and glorious his career, it would have been only marginally relevant for the Presidency. However, Eisenhower was not that kind of soldier. Throughout his military career he was destined never to command troops in battle. His success was due, not to his ability in the field, but to his capacity to plan and co-ordinate complex military operations. So that when the United States entered World War II in December 1941, Eisenhower was soon resigned to the fact that he was likely to spend the war behind a desk. Initially he was assigned to the War Plans Division of the General Staff in Washington as Assistant Chief. By mid-February 1942, following the reorganisation of the Defence Department, he was appointed Assistant Chief of Staff in charge of war plans under General Marshall. In this capacity, Eisenhower was responsible for the preparation of a plan for the invasion of Europe across the English Channel—in rough outline the same plan as that followed on D-Day, two years and three months later. It was this plan which was responsible for Eisenhower's entry into what might be called military diplomacy, for the plan was accepted by the American Government and agreed to in principle by the British. The problems arising from the question of the timing of the opening-up of a second front in Western Europe, which both the U.S.S.R. and public opinion in the West was demanding, led to the need to bring American and British strategic thinking into closer alignment. Eisenhower was chosen to begin this task. He visited London for ten days in May 1942, returning to Washington to draw up a directive for the commander of a European Theatre of Operations. Eisenhower himself was subsequently appointed to this post when President Roosevelt decided that General Marshall, the first choice of both the President and Churchill, could not be spared from Washington.

It is not really surprising that little was known of Eisenhower's career prior to World War II. As a result of the Depression and the consequent government economies, the Army was reduced to fewer than 120,000 men. It was a very small world which suddenly underwent a tremendous upheaval when the Nazis swept across Western Europe in 1940. The fact that in this situation Eisenhower achieved rapid promotion is not in itself surprising. What is remarkable is the fact that an officer so rapidly promoted, who had no experience in actual combat and very little in the command of troops, should be advanced to a position of supreme command over the heads of about 366 regular officers who were senior to him. Eisenhower undoubtedly owed his promotion in the first instance to various General Staff officers, such as General Mark Clark, who recommended him to the Army Chief of Staff, General George Marshall. It is also true that, among Eisenhower's contemporaries, there were very few officers who were temperamentally or otherwise suited for the responsibilities involved in bringing into being the vast new American

7

forces required for the war. However, there was one important factor which influenced Marshall's choice of Commander, a factor which is relevant when it comes to considering Eisenhower's subsequent view of the world when he accepted the Republican nomination for the Presidency. This was his complete agreement with Marshall, the post-war author of the American aid programme for European recovery, on the absolute necessity for a Europe-first strategy. So far as the Pacific was concerned, Eisenhower drew up a plan for his chief the essence of which was for the United States to maintain a holding operation in that area, in order to release the maximum equipment and supplies for the European theatre.

For the remainder of this chapter we need deal only with those aspects of Eisenhower's years as a figure of international repute and importance which are likely to be relevant to the performance of his role as President. If we simply accept the popular view of Eisenhower's wartime experience that he was the principal architect of victory in the West, the principal planner and chief executive of the battles which broke the German Army (Rovere, 1956), then we are likely to accept what seems to be a somewhat mistaken view of Eisenhower the President. Writers such as Sidney Warren and Marquis Childs, who entitle their accounts of his Presidency *Hero in Politics* and *Eisenhower: Captive Hero*, seem to imply that Eisenhower was a good-natured national hero with no preparation for the Presidency. That, inexperienced and uninterested in politics, he was either exploited by unscrupulous politicians for their own ends or was simply too lazy or diffident to play the active role the Presidency requires. If, on the other hand, we consider the view of the journalist A. J. Leibling, who followed the General's activities in North Africa and France, then we have a description of Eisenhower's experience which conforms far more with the duties he performed during the years preceding World War II and his duties (including those at Columbia University) after the war. Liebling described

8

Eisenhower as a political general, a fixer, a chairman-of-the-board sort of commander (Rovere, 1956). For Eisenhower by all accounts was a successful Allied commander not so much because of his military expertise, but because of his skill as a diplomatist.

Two factors in particular seem to have accounted for his success as Supreme Allied Commander in Europe, both of which are relevant for his Presidency. One was his effort to promote Allied harmony. Friction existed, particularly between the American and British Army commanders Bradley and Montgomery, and the Air Force commanders Spaatz and Tedder. Eisenhower was particularly skilful at finding compromises, sometimes at the expense of the dilution of strategy, but political as well as military considerations needed to be taken into account. Eisenhower, according to Rostow, was an admirable director of an Allied staff, understanding particularly well the delicacy of the British transition from senior to junior partner in the European theatre, and making that transition as easy as it could possibly be made for the British (Rostow, 1960).

The second factor which accounted for Eisenhower's wartime success was a conception of the requirements of a modern executive, which generated a view of institutionalised leadership, to be reflected later in his conduct of the office of President. In his war memoirs Eisenhower concludes an analysis of the modern general's task by saying, among other things that,

the teams and staffs through which the modern commander absorbs information and exercises his authority must be a beautifully interlocked, smooth-working mechanism. Ideally, the whole should be practically a single mind (Eisenhower, 1948, i. 74-6).

While this view was particularly useful for an Allied Staff headquarters of the type which Eisenhower headed in Europe, it might well be argued that it was particularly inappropriate for the office of the President. President Truman, for example, is supposed to have remarked that

9

the President makes foreign policy. At the very least this means that the President is intimately involved in the policy-making process. However, Eisenhower's ideas on administration did not preclude the Chief Executive, any less than the general, from being involved in the policy-making process. Rather, the question for Eisenhower was at what level he would enter the process, and this in turn depended on his conception of leadership.

The origins of Eisenhower's ideas on leadership can also be traced to his military career. During World War II especially he exercised ultimate command over men who were not only more directly experienced than himself in warfare, but whose operational skill he also greatly respected. Not having commanded men in battle himself, he had the soldier's respect for officers who had. Thus when his staff achieved agreement among themselves, Eisenhower tended to accept their decision, sometimes against his own instinctive judgement about the course operations should take (Rostow, 1960). His great genius was in finding a compromise solution when his staff could not agree. The extent to which these conceptions influenced Eisenhower's conduct of the Presidency, and to what effect, will be discussed below. Suffice it to say at this stage that as President, Eisenhower's respect for experts did not lead him to accept their judgement over his own in vital areas of foreign and military policy where he was himself especially knowledgeable.

Post-war experience

If Eisenhower's wartime role left him with considerable knowledge and experience in the field of foreign affairs, and particularly in the handling of America's allies, this was consolidated further by his last military appointment prior to his nomination for the Presidency in 1952. In 1949 the North Atlantic Treaty Organisation (N.A.T.O.) was established, and in December 1950 Eisenhower was asked by Truman to become its military commander. Eisenhower was the natural choice because of his wartime experience and popularity among America's allies.

Many commentators have pointed to the similarity between the circumstances surrounding Eisenhower's arrival in Europe to command N.A.T.O. in the autumn of 1950 and his arrival to command the European theatre of operations in 1942. For the United States and her European allies, the world situation in the autumn of 1950 appeared menacing and the outlook for the future dangerous and uncertain. The United Nations forces were maintaining only a precarious foothold on the Korean Peninsula and, in addition to the Communist attack in the Far East, it was sincerely believed in the highest places in Washington that a similar proxy attack, probably by some European Communist state rather than by the U.S.S.R. itself, could be expected on Western Europe. The suddenness of the Korean attack, it was believed, demonstrated the unpreparedness of the Western powers, and a very expensive rearmament programme was embarked upon with great urgency. In 1951 Congress passed a Mutual Security Bill providing $4,700,000,000 for military aid to the N.A.T.O. powers. This, it was widely stated, was the first step in creating the necessary N.A.T.O. infrastructure—pipelines, airfields and other installations linking the Atlantic ports of France with the N.A.T.O. forces in Germany.

As in 1942, Eisenhower arrived in Europe as a symbol of American power and as the confident, reassuring leader of the Western Allies dedicated to the defence of a strong, united Europe. If, in 1942, there were still many Americans who doubted the wisdom of United States' intervention in world affairs, especially in Europe, such feelings were also held in the winter of 1950-1. As N.A.T.O. commander, Eisenhower had not only to convince the European governments of the need for unity, but also to reassure those Americans in the Congress and the country at large of the need for continued American involvement in Europe, in terms of manpower as well as money and equipment. It was at this time that Eisenhower attempted to persuade the isolationist Senator Robert A. Taft that collective security in Europe should be adopted as a definite feature of United States foreign policy, and asked the Senator to support this as a bi-partisan policy. Eisenhower made it clear to Taft that he would renounce any political ambitions he might have if the Senator would agree to this. This offer must have been rather attractive to Taft, in view of his own aspirations for the Republican nomination for 1952. However, he refused, and the division in American opinion which Taft's refusal reflected was, as the next chapter will explain, a major factor in persuading Eisenhower to run for President himself.

One of his principal tasks on taking up his appointment was to secure agreement among the N.A.T.O. members on a plan for bringing West German forces into the Western defence system. The plan which Eisenhower was urging on the Europeans was the French proposal for a European Defence Community (E.D.C.), by which West Germany, France, Italy, Belgium, the Netherlands and Luxembourg would set up a supranational army, with a common uniform and budget, to serve within N.A.T.O. Eisenhower's principal political problem was to reconcile the important differences which existed among the European countries, and in particular the French fear of German rearmament. During his two years of duty in Paris, he was brought into frequent contact with the governments that were reluctant to sign the agreement, trying, without very much success it is true, to convince them that the integration principle would mean that no one country's forces would be self-sufficient, independent of the whole—not even those of the United States.

The E.D.C. issue apart, Eisenhower was not unsuccessful. He got on extremely well with such European leaders as Jean Monnet, Paul-Henri Spaak, Rene Pleven, Joseph Bech (of Luxembourg), Bevin and Attlee. With the Continental Europeans Eisenhower was on especially amicable terms, largely because he both singled out and was singled out by those who shared his commitment to the idea of European unity. By May 1952 Eisenhower had completed the establishment and organisation of the N.A.T.O. H.Q. and had secured the signatures of all the member nations, including France, to the protocol for the international military organisation and unified commands. Thus, parallel to its obvious military nature, Eisenhower's role at N.A.T.O. had its complex political character. Few other Presidential candidates in American history had this experience or were able to acquire this familiarity with so essential a component of United States foreign and defence policy.

This rather brief analysis of Eisenhower's career prior to the 1952 election is essential to any understanding of the Eisenhower Presidency. For, apart from its obvious implications for his conceptions of leadership and organisational principle, it accounts also for his internationalist outlook and, consequently, as the following chapter will show, his conception of his role as President in respect of foreign affairs. Moreover, it shows also that in some significant aspects of the Presidency, again particularly in foreign and military matters, Eisenhower was not a novice when he took office.

2

Eisenhower's conception of his role as President

In this chapter Eisenhower's conception of his role as President is examined, with particular reference to his understanding of the requirements of American foreign policy when he took office. Furthermore, we need to consider also his conception of his role in domestic affairs. Eisenhower was not unaware of the essential interdependence between domestic politics and foreign policy decisions. He nevertheless distinguished between his constitutional position in foreign as opposed to domestic matters.

Domestic affairs

Conferring with members of his future Cabinet on board the U.S.S. *Helena*, when returning from his brief pre-Inaugural visit to Korea in December 1952, Eisenhower stated some of his own ideas. He did not think of the office of the Presidency as Roosevelt and Truman had done,

> but according to an older conception—the Executive as one of the three equal branches of the government, who was not trying to do too much leading. . . . The government's role in domestic affairs was to assure fair play, not to attempt to direct the national economic life (Goldman, 1962, i. 237).

The problem, as he had stated it some months previously

during the election campaign, was 'to achieve a balance which would assure individual liberty in an orderly society' (Eisenhower, I, 1963, i. 51). This balance was his famous middle way, for 'we had to recognise our responsibility to those in real need and alleviate their suffering by the aid of private and local institutions; if the job was too big for those institutions, then the government must help' (Eisenhower I, 1963, i. 51). Big government, however, was not the solution. 'The only way we could achieve . . . the full potential of each individual in an environment of freedom, was to pursue tirelessly the course our forefathers proposed—the middle way' (Eisenhower, I, 1963, i. 7).

Platitudinous as these—and indeed most of Eisenhower's —statements of his beliefs were, they nevertheless provide a fairly accurate guide to his conception of his role in domestic affairs. For if Eisenhower had a political philosophy, it was, as he himself admitted, a basically conservative one and there is very little evidence to suggest that he conceived of his role, *vis-à-vis* domestic affairs, as being very much more than to assure fair play. Nor, indeed, did it oblige him to be a politician, or even to be involved in politics, in the way that Presidents Roosevelt, Truman or Kennedy were. He was not a politician seeking power for himself or, for that matter, his party. For, as it has often been pointed out, Eisenhower genuinely believed that the Presidency was, or ought to be, above politics: that it ought to be a source of unifying, moderating influence, above the struggle, on the model of George Washington. For example, at a Press conference in late 1953, a reporter asked whether Eisenhower planned to participate in the 1954 Congressional campaign. His reply was characteristic. Although he said he was deeply interested in the make-up of the Senate and the House of Representatives, he insisted that he did 'not intend to make of the Presidency an agency to use in partisan elections . . . anybody occupying this office is President of all the people' and must develop a programme of benefit to everyone:

> I have no intention of going out and getting into partisan struggles in any district or in any state because I know that I, for one, in such a state would resent that kind of intrusion from the President of the United States (*Presidential Papers*, 1953).

Foreign affairs

To understand Eisenhower's conception of his role in this sphere we need to see why he accepted the Republican nomination for the Presidency, given his obvious distaste for practical politics and his apparent lack of knowledge of and interest in domestic affairs. Eisenhower was always most particular to stress his conviction that

> the necessary and wise subordination of the military to civil power will be best sustained . . . when lifelong professional soldiers, in the absence of some obvious and overriding reasons, abstain from seeking high political office (Eisenhower, I, 1963, i. 7).

What, then, were the obvious and overriding reasons which caused him to actively seek the Presidency? Broadly, it seems, Eisenhower accepted the Presidential nomination because he was persuaded that he was the only person who could sustain the national consensus established by Roosevelt on domestic, but, above all, on foreign policy. Maintained by Truman in the early years of his Presidency, the political consensus was endangered by the American involvement in Korea, the chief symbol of the frustratingly indecisive Cold War.

The national mood in 1952

It is worth recalling the 'national mood' in the United States at the beginning of the 1950's, for it has direct bearing on Eisenhower's view of his role as President. Parallel with the consensus on domestic affairs, which had emerged out of the political struggles of the New Deal period, there
16

was, by 1950, a well-established consensus on foreign policy. The latter too owed its growth to the Roosevelt era. In the early years of World War II, the President sought to consolidate a bi-partisan foreign policy, based on the internationalist position he adopted in 1940-1 and which led to the creation, in 1942, of the Atlantic Alliance. However, it was left to President Truman to lead the United States into the United Nations and, in collaboration with Republicans like Senator Vandenberg, to carry through measures such as the Marshall Plan, the Greek-Turkish aid programme, the Berlin Airlift and the Point 4 Programme for aiding the underdeveloped areas. The foreign-policy consensus rested on the concept of containment: put very briefly, it was generally accepted that by resisting all forms of Soviet aggression, by maintaining and increasing the military and economic strength of the West, and by preventing the neutral, underdeveloped countries from going Communist, it would be possible to avoid a third world war and to allow the resolution of the Cold War to be worked out slowly over a period of some years.

The foreign-policy consensus of Roosevelt and Truman was seriously jeopardised by the entry of the Chinese into the Korean War in November 1950, when the early victories of what was ostensibly a United Nations force, but was in reality an American expedition, were dramatically reversed. The consequent defeats, the capture of thousands of American troops and the eventual stalemate in the fighting aroused profound popular dissatisfaction in the United States against the Administration's adherence to what seemed a protracted, over-cautious and evidently unsuccessful policy of containment.

There was, first, a brief yet significant resurgence of the old isolationist tendencies in the wake of the disastrous defeats of December 1950. However, the idea of getting out of Korea and leaving the Asian mainland to the Chinese was abandoned once the American forces rallied and General Ridgeway was able to stabilise the military situation.

Second, there was the alternative, of which General MacArthur was to become the champion, of breaking out of the dilemmas of the containment policy by adopting a more adventurous, aggressive course. A range of alternative actions were proposed, from the bombing of Manchuria to launching a preventive war against China. To MacArthur, limited warfare was simply the appeasement of Communism. The result was prolonged indecision, since 'in war there is no substitute for victory' (Goldman, 1962, i. 208). The popularity of this alternative to containment reached its height during MacArthur's triumphant tour of the United States, following the General's dismissal by President Truman from the command of the United Nations forces in Korea. It began to fade, however, during the Senate hearings on the case, when the Administration, largely through the Joint Chiefs of Staff, began to take the offensive against the General.

Third, the consensus foreign policy was attacked by such men as Senators McCarthy, Jenner and Knowland, who argued that the real source of danger to the United States was treason from within. So far as international affairs were concerned, McCarthyism placed a relatively low appreciation on the importance of Soviet economic and military power *vis-à-vis* that of the United States, and instead inflated enormously the threat of Soviet espionage and political infiltration inside America. The deprecation of Soviet power, as William V. Shannon has pointed out, appealed to those who liked to think of American power as unchallengeable. The exaggeration of Communist subversion catered to a range of xenophobic and populist notions about foreigners, radicals and Communists (Shannon, 1958). McCarthyism was only beginning in 1950; it was not to lose its force for more than four years.

President Truman and his Secretary of State, Dean Acheson, proved to be relatively ineffective defenders of the containment policy, of which they were the chief architects and exponents. The fundamental dissatisfaction with foreign affairs manifested itself in a violent anti-

Trumanism, particularly on the issue of Far-Eastern policy. Against mounting virulent attacks from the Republican Party, and in particular from Senator Taft and the Mc-Carthyites, Truman and Acheson could only repeat the familiar and tired arguments about collective security, the United Nations and the importance of having allies. Neither had the stature, ability or style to counter-attack effectively.

The military ethos

It was against this background that Eisenhower entered politics, having, it is suggested here, a relatively clear idea of the role he was to play. If he brought to the Presidency his military conceptions of organisation and method, he brought to it also a certain military ethos—namely, the placing of a high value on national unity and a high regard for the *status quo*, which the soldier is trained to defend. In preferring the conservative Republicans, with their dedication to preserving the *status quo* over the traditionally reformist Democrats, Eisenhower seems to have been true to the military ethic. Indeed, in this connection it is particularly important to remember that Eisenhower had actually been offered the Presidential nominations of both the Republican and the Democratic Parties from 1948 or even earlier. Since he had undoubtedly supported the Roosevelt-Truman foreign policies (the most important parts of his career—during World War II, as Army Chief of Staff from 1945-7, and at N.A.T.O.—had been carried on in intimate association with the Democratic Presidents), and since he accepted, in opposition to Senator Taft, the nomination of the internationalist wing of the Republican Party, we can only assume that his choice was determined by his preference for the Republican's domestic conservatism.

The maintenance of internationalism

In late 1949 Senator Arthur Vandenberg wrote in a private

letter to a friend that he might support Eisenhower in the next Presidential Election: 'I think the specifications call for a personality of great independent magnitude who can give our splintering American people an evangel instead of an ordinary campaign' (Shannon, 1959, i. 393). The 1952 campaign could hardly have been considered an 'evangel' by anybody's standards, but there was in Eisenhower's attitude towards the role of President a sense of mission. As nominee of the more moderate Republicans interested in preserving the foreign-policy consensus, he had been persuaded that as President he would only be carrying out his N.A.T.O. assignment in a different way. For by forestalling the nomination of Senator Taft and preventing the coming to power of the Senator's neo-isolationalist backers, Eisenhower would make certain that a foreign policy oriented towards the defence of Europe and the maintenance of the United Nations would continue to prevail. Nevertheless, it is important to note, as Richard Rovere has pointed out, that it was not only for the negative reason of forestalling Senator Taft that Eisenhower agreed to stand for the Presidency. It was also because he saw his Presidential role as the continuation of his roles at the Supreme H.Q. Allied Expeditionary Forces (S.H.A.E.F.) and the Supreme H.Q. Allied Powers Europe (S.H.A.P.E.)—namely, as the great unifier, the leader in war and peace of the coalition of Western democracies.

Eisenhower, in his memoirs, describes a significant visit to him at N.A.T.O. H.Q. in September 1951 by the then Senator, Henry Cabot Lodge, Jr. The General was obviously impressed by the Senator's arguments, and, although he only promised to think over the matter, he subsequently saw the visit as a turning-point in his decision to accept the Republican nomination.

'The Republican Party,' Lodge told him, 'must now seek to nominate one who, supporting basic Republican convictions—which had come down to us from Lincoln and Theodore Roosevelt—could be elected and achieve at least a partial reversal of the trend towards centralisation in government, irresponsible spending, and catering to pressure groups, and *at the same time avoid the fatal errors of isolationism*' (Eisenhower, I, 1963, i. 18).

It was to a very similar appeal that Eisenhower was particularly responsive in 1956, when he was being urged to run for a second term. According to Robert Donovan, Eisenhower by then felt he was under very little obligation to the leaders of the Republican Party to run again. The urgings to which he responded were those of his friends, advisers and the Press, reminding him of the uniqueness of his position as being 'the right man in the right place at the right time to deal with one issue which towers above all others—the cause of peace or war' (Donovan, 1956, i. 402).

Constitutional view of the Presidency

It will be clear from what has been said so far that Eisenhower's conception of his role precluded that he view it as did President Wilson, writing in an academic treatise in 1907:

'The President is at liberty both in law and conscience to be as big a man as he can. His capacity,' Wilson wrote, 'will set the limit, and if Congress be overborne by him, it will be no fault of the makers of the Constitution—it will be from no lack of constitutional powers on its part, but only because the President has the nation behind him, and the Congress has not' (Warren, 1964, i. 65).

Few Presidents have been so fortunate as to have had the nation behind them to the extent that Eisenhower had. He won overwhelming personal majorities in both the 1952 and, particularly, the 1956 campaigns. On the other hand, few Presidents, and none of the modern ones, have exploited their popularity less than Eisenhower. To some extent this might have been due to diffidence towards politics, laziness, or distaste for this aspect of the Presidency. But the fact that he actively sought the nomination and fought for the Presidency twice, when he might have retired comfortably to spend all his time at golf or bridge, suggests that Eisenhower did believe that he had a definite role to fulfil.

For the suggestion here is that it was not solely due to laziness or diffidence, to his lack of experience or even ability, that prevented Eisenhower from pursuing the active personal leadership and innovational role in the political process pursued by Roosevelt, Truman or Kennedy. Rather it was due to his basically conservative view of his role. In the next section, Eisenhower's conception of the 'institutionalised Presidency' will be examined. In this chapter, however, we have noted above that Eisenhower believed that the government had only a minimal role to play in domestic affairs. Richard Rovere has remarked that the parts of his Administration that dealt with domestic affairs were virtually autonomous, while in most matters that concerned major issues of war and peace Eisenhower held on to his powers of decision very firmly. While this latter point too is the subject of a later chapter of this study, what is being suggested here is that this too was not solely due to the fact that Eisenhower was interested and/or experienced in foreign affairs and had neither interest nor experience in domestic matters. Instead, it is suggested that this distinction was consistent with Eisenhower's constitutional view of the Presidency. So far as domestic matters were concerned, the question of States' Rights, the separation of powers and other constitutional provisions, precluded that Eisenhower take so broad a view of his powers as that taken by President Wilson in 1907. In foreign affairs, on the other hand, the Constitution specifically entrusts primary responsibility to the President, and, as will be seen below, this was not a responsibility that he shirked, so long as his state of health permitted.

3

Eisenhower's Administration

Eisenhower's conception of 'orderly administration'

In his memoirs, Eisenhower expresses his amazement at those who 'seem to suggest that smooth organisation guarantees that nothing is happening, whereas ferment and disorder indicate progress' (Eisenhower, I, 1963, i. 114). In the minds of most commentators, nothing characterises the Eisenhower Presidency more than the President's use of the staff system and his conception of orderly administration. Rostow, for example, writes of Eisenhower's idealised view of bureaucratic leadership (Rostow, 1960), which, as was suggested in the first chapter of this study, can be said to have been derived from his somewhat unusual military experience.

Most critical studies of the Eisenhower Presidency make the President's ideas about organisation a major factor in explaining the apparent slow pace of innovation by his Administration and its sluggish response to new situations. There is, unquestionably, a great deal of validity in this argument. However, in the light of the analysis undertaken in this study, some modification of this opinion is warranted. In particular, it will be suggested here that E. S. Corwin's (Corwin, 1957) contention that, under Eisenhower, tendencies towards the bureaucratisation of the Presidency became *controlling* is in need of some qualification, particularly when considering the Administration's foreign policy.

At the outset it must be said that the Roosevelt style of competing subordinates and advisers, with overlapping jurisdictions, were an anathema to Eisenhower and his conception of orderly administration. For example, it is characteristic of Eisenhower that he should emphasise that part of the cause of the 1961 Bay of Pigs fiasco was 'inefficient functioning of governmental organisation, bringing about indecision and untimely counter-orders' (Eisenhower, II, 1965, i. 631). It was equally characteristic of President Kennedy's biographers to place the blame principally on the fact that, being new to office, Kennedy was obliged to heed the advice of anonymous experts. Both were probably correct, but their different emphases are significant.

In this chapter we shall be mainly concerned with two questions arising out of Eisenhower's view of administration. The first concerns the delegation of responsibility; the second the question of the President's access to information. At the end of the chapter we shall consider Eisenhower's relations with Congress and the Republican Party. The first question involves, among other things, consideration of the position of Sherman Adams, whose role in the office of the President was equivalent to that of an army chief of staff. It involves too, consideration of the extent to which Eisenhower's use of the Cabinet and the White House Staff, his great respect for, and apparent reliance upon, the opinions of experts, and above all his apparent dedication to consensus both within and outside his Administration determined his actions with respect to foreign policy-making. Did Eisenhower's conception of an institutionalised Presidency in effect mean the total delegation of his decision-making powers to a bureaucracy?

The second question, that of Eisenhower's access to information, needs to be related to his interests and intellectual ability. One of Eisenhower's greatest political assets was his ability to appear as a dignified 'father-figure' on the one hand, while at the same time remaining always a simple man, 'a man to like, an individual of immense goodwill, great warmth with people, slight interest in politics, paltry regard for ideas [and] no sensitivity to words' (Hughes, 1963, i. 148). This view of Eisenhower, from a man who knew him fairly well during his Presidency, highlights a very important fact about him : namely, his lack of intellectual interests. Sherman Adams noted that Eisenhower was not much of a reader. He glanced at several newspapers every morning, but paid little attention to those that continually attacked him. Furthermore, Eisenhower seldom read the Washington papers, arguing that they did not tell you 'how the people feel about things' (Adams, 1962, i. 70). As opposed to President Kennedy, therefore, who is described by one of his biographers as a fanatical reader— 1,200 words a minute—or President Roosevelt, who went through vast quantities of official documents and many newspapers, Eisenhower read little, and was impatient with the endless paper-work of the Presidency. He always tried to get his staff to digest long documents into one-page summaries, which, as Sherman Adams comments, was sometimes an impossible task (Adams, 1962). He did, however, subject correspondence addressed to him personally to close scrutiny, and throughout his Presidency correspond regularly with a number of friends and acquaintances, some of whom were in a position to offer him valuable information and advice.

Therefore, in considering the extent to which Eisenhower's conception of an institutionalised Presidency involved the total delegation of his decision-making powers to a bureaucracy, it is necessary to consider also the extent to which the bureaucracy circumscribed his sources of information, leaving him either uninformed or misinformed on important matters. In other words, was Eisenhower the prisoner of his conception of an institutionalised Presidency to the extent that it prevented him from applying his own views and understanding in foreign policy-making?

The delegation of responsibility

In answering these questions it is necessary to distinguish between foreign and domestic policy. This is not because it is being suggested here that nowadays such a distinction is possible in substance. Rather it is because, as was seen in the previous chapter, Eisenhower had a somewhat different view of his role in each of the two spheres, and also because, however much they may overlap, different institutions and personalities are involved. In the domestic sphere, Eisenhower's establishment of a staff system achieved a degree of administrative orderliness in the White House far superior to that of other modern Administrations. Basically, the system hinged upon the Assistant to the President, Sherman Adams. Because his duties were so broad and general, and because Eisenhower himself never defined precisely his responsibilities or outlined their limits, Adams became known variously as the Assistant President and the 'second most powerful executive in the government' (Adams, 1962, i. 56). However, it does seem wrong to assume that Adams was very much more than an administrator, a chief of staff who fulfilled for Eisenhower functions closely analagous to those carried out by Bedell Smith, Clay and Gruenther during the President's military career.

Adams himself has described his duties as being,

to manage a staff that would simplify and expedite the urgent business that had to be brought to his [the President's] personal attention and to keep as much work of secondary importance as possible off his desk (Adams, 1962, i. 56).

This unquestionably gave him great power, for it suggests that it was Adams and his staff, and not the President, who determined where and on what issues the Administration should act, thereby determining also the type of decisions the President would make in the domestic sphere. On the other hand, it is equally important to point out that there
26

is evidence to suggest that one should not ascribe too much power to Sherman Adams. Emmet Hughes notes that Adams rarely if ever attempted to work as a policy-maker, and Adams himself once remarked that he conceived his role in the White House 'as scrubbing the administrative and political backstairs' (Hughes, 1963, i. 64). In his zeal to protect Eisenhower, especially from Senators and Congressmen seeking favours, and thereby allow the President more time for higher policy matters, Adams probably insulated him from many sources of information. However, this was conceivably of no great consequence, when measured against what is sometimes believed to be his most valuable role as a convenient whipping-boy for Eisenhower. Moreover, although Adams was a former Governor of New Hampshire, he did not enjoy any significant degree of political support in the country at large, and even less in Washington. Thus his somewhat vulnerable political position and his position within the Administration hierarchy made him and not Eisenhower the target for hostile critics in the Republican Party, while the President was able to maintain his father-figure image above politics.

The Eisenhower Administration

At this stage it is worth taking a closer look at Eisenhower's ideas on government and comparing them with those of President Kennedy. The heart of the Eisenhower system was staff work. With Sherman Adams at the top as chief of staff, several staffs or groups existed to deal with different fields of policy-making. Sometimes these groups met with the President all together, but usually he dealt with them separately, with Adams acting as co-ordinator. One group, for example, served to promote Eisenhower's legislative programme; in the field of economic policy there was the Council of Economic Advisers and the Bureau of the Budget, with their respective staffs. Several members of the White House Staff were given unique posts; for example, when the Foreign Operations Administration was incorporated in the State Department in 1955, its first Director was Harold E. Stassen. A former Governor of Minnesota and a perennial candidate for the Republican Party's Presidential nomination, he was given the official title of Special Assistant to the President with the principal task of co-ordinating the Administration's policies in the field of disarmament.

Under Eisenhower, the Cabinet was accorded unique prominence as a consultative body; in addition to the secretaries, it comprised presidential assistants and directors of important agencies on whom Eisenhower conferred Cabinet rank and status. They included, among others, the United States Ambassador to the United Nations (Henry Cabot Lodge, Jr.), the Director of Defence Mobilisation, the Director of the Budget Bureau, the Director of Mutual Security, the Assistant to the President for national security affairs, the Special Assistant in charge of Cold War psychology planning, and Sherman Adams. Eisenhower, according to Adams, never made a policy decision on an important domestic issue until his course of action had been talked over and supported at a Cabinet meeting. Foreign-policy issues were discussed first by the National Security Council, but in this field, too, significant new problems were reviewed in the Cabinet. At the well-reported first Cabinet meeting held at the Commodore Hotel in New York, a week before his Inauguration, Eisenhower announced that

> No one of you, whether a Cabinet member or one who functions as such, is relieved of his part of the responsibility for making government policy. No major decisions will be made by the National Security Council but what will be reviewed by the Cabinet and brought back to the N.S.C. (Adams, 1962, i. 19).

Thus it seems that each member of the Cabinet was expected to discuss any question that the government happened to be deliberating at the moment. But the arrangements for and the actual Cabinet meetings themselves were characterised by an uncommon degree of formality. Under

28

the Secretary to the Cabinet, Maxwell M. Rabb, elaborate policy papers were prepared in advance for each item to be discussed. The meetings were held regularly each week, with the members who were due to present items of departmental business to the Cabinet being carefully rehearsed by the Secretary, sometimes going over their statements three or more times until they achieved perfect timing.

The same rigid formality characterised the meetings of the National Security Council, the main forum for the discussion of foreign-policy issues. There was, however, very little discussion of alternative policies, since the process of reconciling different views took place in the Council's Planning Board. It was here, in the Planning Board, that the view was most clearly discernible that 'policy should be made by achieving an acceptable consensus among all those operationally responsible for, or even interested in, the outcome' (Rostow, 1960, i. 386). Eisenhower's conservative views on change—that it must be gradual, based on consensus, rather than radical, achieved by struggle or conflict—appear to have been extended to the very heart of the Federal bureaucracy. In a speech to the National War College in June 1957 Secretary of Defence Wilson declared:

> Our government is a government of checks and balances. The President cannot do certain things without checking with the Congress. Within the Executive branch, policies are co-ordinated with all the departments concerned, and decisions are reached after all have had their say. We follow the same procedure within the Department of Defence. . . . The final decision will not always completely satisfy everybody concerned. In an organisation composed of people working for a common purpose, decisions are accepted in the knowledge that they were reached after full consideration of all points of view (Rostow, 1960, i. 386).

The Kennedy Administration

If President Eisenhower appears to have leaned heavily on

staff counsel and collective judgement, leaving his policy decisions until differences of opinion had been resolved, President Kennedy appears to have brought an entirely different conception of administration and policy-making to his office. He abandoned the practice of the Cabinet and National Security Council making group decisions, and abolished the weekly Cabinet meetings. He abolished also the pyramid structure of the White House Staff, Sherman Adam's job, the Staff Secretary, the Cabinet Secretariat and the N.S.C. Planning Board, 'all of which imposed, in his view, needless paper-work and machinery between the President and his responsible officers' (Sorensen, 1965, i. 314). Kennedy believed that the elaborate Eisenhower system diluted and distributed his authority, and he was not interested in the unanimous decisions of committees which rested upon the lowest common denominators of compromise.

Here then, we are to assume, is the ideal type of the active as opposed to the passive President. The active Kennedy relying on

> informal meetings and direct contacts . . . on a personal staff, the Budget Bureau and *ad hoc* task forces to probe and define issues for his decision . . . on special Presidential emissaries and constant Presidential phone calls and memoranda—on placing Kennedy men in each strategic spot (Sorensen, 1965, i. 314).

(Eisenhower, incidentally, disliked using the telephone for conducting business. The only person in the government who did have frequent phone conversations with him was Dulles. All other Cabinet officers and agency directors came to his office and spoke to him there, or else conducted their business through Adams and his staff. Even Adams, who apparently made some 250 phone calls each day, rarely spoke to the President on the telephone, and then only on matters that required 'yes/no' answers.)

Under Kennedy the Cabinet as an institution was reduced to virtual insignificance, convened, according to Sorensen, largely as a symbol to be informed, not consulted (Sorensen, 1965). Kennedy also apparently had little interest in the views of Cabinet members on matters outside their departmental jurisdictions. McNamara, the Secretary of Defence, was asked to advise in the steel price dispute of 1962 because he had formerly been President of the Ford Motor Co., just as Douglas Dillon of the Treasury would be included on most major foreign-policy issues. However, Kennedy did not believe, according to Sorensen, that McNamara could offer him any worthwhile advice on debt-management, nor could Dillon, say, on the question of the development of the Nike-Zeus missile systems.

Finally, the National Security Council under Kennedy remained on much more formal and organised a basis than the Cabinet, but the President was always concerned to let it be known that *he* ran its meetings. He was also most careful to make it clear, as he did at a Press conference in 1961, that, in contrast to Eisenhower, he placed a low value on the Council as a body in which it was possible to decide anything of consequence. He preferred instead to operate directly with far fewer people, such as the Secretaries of Defence and State, McGeorge Bundy, the head of the C.I.A. and the Vice-President—the nucleus, incidentally, of the Excomm., the Executive Committee of the N.S.C., which handled the Cuba missile crisis of 1962.

Evaluation

This necessarily brief and idealised comparison between the Eisenhower and Kennedy conceptions of government and administration has been included here to illustrate the very real extent to which Eisenhower was *sui-generis*, since Kennedy obviously had far more in common with the other modern Presidents.

Nevertheless, however passive Eisenhower's conception of his office obliged him to be, we should not assume that he was its helpless prisoner, particularly with regard to foreign policy. His system obviously had its failings. For example, no position or function equivalent to that of Sherman Adams in respect of domestic affairs emerged in the foreign-policy field, although Eisenhower did urge the appointment of a Secretary for International Co-ordination upon his successor, who ignored it. The problem was principally one of co-ordination. As Eisenhower himself put it:

> In earlier, simpler days, all foreign affairs of our government were co-ordinated under the immediate supervision of the Secretary of State, while the President, in fulfilling his constitutional responsibility for foreign relations, could work almost exclusively with the Secretary. Our popular concept . . . still lingers, even though a host of informational, trade, financial, military and other matters now affecting our relations abroad are not under the jurisdiction of the Secretary of State (Eisenhower, II, 1965, i. 637).

The Eisenhower-Dulles relationship will be discussed below, but here it must be pointed out that the Secretary of State's limited view of his role ruled out the possibility that he would act so as to co-ordinate diplomacy, military affairs, economic foreign policy, propaganda and all the other instruments of American foreign policy. Eisenhower, indeed, consulted Dulles about making such an appointment, but Dulles opposed it, even when Eisenhower told him that he had him in mind for the job. As Eisenhower puts it:

> it was inconceivable to him that anyone other than the Secretary of State could have the right to speak to or for the President on any matter involving international affairs, even though the matter might fall legally outside the purview of his own responsibility (Eisenhower, II, 1965, i. 637).

The Secretary of Defence and the Joint Chiefs of Staff guarded their prerogatives just as jealously and there was clearly no one on the White House staff with the political and administrative weight to be able to come between these powerful personages and the President. Consequently, considerable and not-too-well co-ordinated powers remained in the hands of the Cabinet officers. Nevertheless, it must be said that co-ordination was not a particularly strong point in the Kennedy Administration. For example, even Sorensen is obliged to describe the advice on policy, or attendance at conferences in Latin America, by a host of New Frontiersmen, in addition to the usual foreign policy and foreign aid officers, as 'producing some dismay among the State Department professionals and some disarray in the continuity of policy' (Sorensen, 1965, i. 590).

In evaluating the Eisenhower system of government, a few important points must be remembered. As the first chapter of this study attempted to show, Eisenhower by intent and inclination was a *laissez-faire* President. So far as domestic matters were concerned, he conceived of government as meaning orderly administration, and under Sherman Adams and his successor, General Wilton Persons, his Administration was entirely orderly. However, whatever his views on the Cabinet and the decision-making process may suggest in terms of staff or committee decisions, leaving him to act as a cypher or rubber stamp, Eisenhower has been very insistent that he has always believed in the principle that the ultimate decision rests with the leader. In his memoirs, Eisenhower remarks that in this matter the Presidency does not operate any differently from the time in the Civil War, when, on a crucial issue, Lincoln called for a vote around the Cabinet table : 'Every member voted no. "The ayes have it," Lincoln announced' (Eisenhower I, 1963, i. 115). Later, in his account of his Presidency, Eisenhower ridicules the idea that any decision could possibly have been reached in a body which included such diverse personalities as Dulles, Wilson, Benson, Lodge, Stassen and Secretary of the Treasury Humphrey. He himself would always have to decide. In truth, however, it meant also that decisions were very slow to be taken and policy initiatives were relatively rare. However, it is one of the main contentions of this study that this was inherent in Eisenhower's conception of his role. His Administration was very well attuned to his belief that the United States could best solve its problems and protect its interests by slow, gradual change in the classic American manner.

Access to information

A second point which must be made about Eisenhower's administrative system concerns the apparent way it operated to limit the information and diversity of advice that reached the President. As has already been pointed out, Eisenhower read relatively little. On the face of it, his information concerning policy matters reached him in the form of one-page digests that had been processed through the staff system. So far as foreign policy and defence matters were concerned, he seemed to rely heavily on oral briefings from only a few sources : in the former case from Dulles, in the latter from the Special Assistant to the President for National Security Affairs, a position held by Robert Cutler and others during his Presidency. Nevertheless, there were a few important foreign policy initiatives during his term of office for which Eisenhower personally seems to have been responsible. There were, more significantly, important occasions on which Eisenhower overruled Dulles, and it is by no means clear who dominated whom. For it appears to be something more than a conjecture to say that, despite the undoubted influence and dominating position of Dulles, he was very far from being the only source of information and advice available to the President on foreign affairs.

Eisenhower suffered from neither depression nor isolation in his office. He surrounded himself with a large coterie of unofficial advisers and a great number of companions, with whom he fished, played golf or bridge. Probably the man who was closest to him was his brother, Dr. Milton Eisenhower, President of Pennsylvania State College when Eisenhower took office and subsequently of

34

Johns Hopkins University. Milton Eisenhower had an office suite in the old State Department building and worked there nearly every week-end, when an Army plane took him to Washington. His functions included speech-writing, preparing recommendations for the reorganisation of an executive bureau and carrying out fact-finding or goodwill tours of Latin America. Moreover, Donovan reports, that while Milton offered his brother advice in only a few particular fields, he listened to the President and let him work his thoughts out on him. 'Sometimes,' Donovan says, '. . . the two will sit together in the President's bedroom for hours while the President grinds out his ideas on different subjects' (Donovan, 1956, i.197). Other close advisers were Generals Alfred M. Gruenther and Walter Bedell Smith. The latter enjoyed a special status beyond his official post as Under-Secretary of State, communicating with the President directly by means of a special telephone in his business office even after he retired from public service. Gruenther had been Eisenhower's chief of staff at N.A.T.O., and had been seriously considered for Sherman Adam's job as Assistant to the President. In a conversation with Emmet Hughes in October 1957, Eisenhower expressed his great admiration for Gruenther, who became N.A.T.O. Supreme Commander in succession to General Ridgeway in 1953 : 'If he were not a soldier *and* a Catholic . . . I'd be for him taking over this spot right here in 1960. . . . How I'd like to roll up my sleeves and go to work for him' (Hughes, 1963, i.252). So long as he remained at S.H.A.P.E., Gruenther was certainly in a position to provide Eisenhower with information on a wide range of military and foreign affairs.

Finally, in this connection, Eisenhower chose as golfing and fishing companions a group of men from the world of big business and finance with whom he became acquainted after he entered politics. These included presidents or officers of such corporations as Chase Manhattan Bank, Coca-Cola, General Electric, Standard Oil and U.S. Steel. The important point about these people was that they represented powerful interests within the internationalist wing of the Republican Party, and had all backed Eisenhower's candidacy. Thus it seems that in foreign affairs, if not on domestic issues, Eisenhower was very far from having to rely on his elaborate staff system for information and ideas.

Relations with Congress and the Republican Party

A further point which requires examination in evaluating Eisenhower's conception of government was his relationship with the Congress and the Republican Party. For no aspect of his Presidency has Eisenhower been criticised more, even by some of his admirers, than his failure to use the full powers of his office and his popularity to influence Congress and dominate and rejuvenate the Republican Party. With respect to the former, Eisenhower's attitude was based deliberately, and for better or worse, consistently, on his view of the Constitution and leadership. For Eisenhower, leadership meant clearly 'persuasion—and conciliation—and education—and patience' (Hughes, 1963, i.124). At S.H.A.E.F. and N.A.T.O. he had excelled at conciliation and compromise. So long as men were reasonable and rational, they should be able to compromise, and he would always be ready to meet anyone halfway. In 1957 he said at a Press conference:

> I, as you know, never employ threats, I never try to hold up clubs of any kind. I just say, 'This is what I believe to be best for the United States,' and I try to convince people by the logic of my position. If that is wrong politically, well then, I suppose you will just have to say I am wrong. (*Presidential Papers*, 1957, i. 591).

So far as relations with Congress were concerned, he believed that Roosevelt and Truman had upset the proper equilibrium between the two branches of government, aggrandising the Executive over the Legislature. His attitude was summed up by a friend as follows:

> Mr. Eisenhower holds firmly to his constitutional concep-
> tion that the Chief Executive should not dominate the
> legislative branch. He believes in [the] separation of
> powers. He would not bludgeon Congress even if he
> could because he thinks it important to preserve a
> balance of powers (Warren, 1964, i. 366).

Eisenhower did, of course, establish a fairly elaborate
machinery for encouraging co-operation between the
Executive and Congress. He was well aware of the strong
oppositionist habits among Congressmen, particularly the
members of his own party; none of the Senators and only
fifteen out of 221 Republican House members had ever
served under a Republican President. However, Eisenhower
soon found the task of conciliation and compromise with
the Congressional leaders an exceedingly hard chore. The
influential Republicans in Congress were largely conservatives who had done nothing to help Eisenhower get the
nomination, nor did they feel any obligation towards him
for having led the Party back to power (Adams, 1962).
Consequently, Eisenhower often found it easier to deal
with the Democrats in Congress (he was obliged to do so
after the Democratic victories in 1954), particularly in
respect of foreign affairs. Indeed, Eisenhower eventually
avoided discussing major decisions with the Republicans in
Congress until he and Dulles had laid out their policies at a
meeting of the leaders of both parties. The implications for
foreign policy of Eisenhower's views on Executive-
Congressional relations will be considered within the context of the discussion in the following chapter. At this
stage it is only necessary to point out that, by refusing to
take an active leadership role, Eisenhower was unable to
ensure that the more moderate Republicans in Congress
would prevail over the strongly entrenched and more
senior ultra-conservatives.

Eventually it meant virtually abandoning, not only
control of Congress, but also the possibility of any
considerable degree of co-operation with it. But, as has
already been pointed out, Eisenhower's conception of the

Presidency precluded that he view it as a centre of political activity or that he should be obliged to be an active political leader. He was so detached from the party whose nomination he had accepted that at one stage, when he realised that the Democrats were more willing to support his foreign policies than the Republicans, he thought seriously about creating a new political party—'accepting a role of leadership in world affairs, liberal in its policies affecting human welfare, but taking a more conservative stand than the Democrats on domestic government controls and spending . . .' (Adams, 1962, i 39).

Moreover, Eisenhower's conception of relations with the Legislature and his relationship with the Republican Party operated to stultify his military and foreign-policy initiatives only to a certain extent, and on the whole he did not allow them to destroy his purpose of keeping to the established course of internationalism and collective security. As the subsequent chapter will show, he was always able to avoid the extremes of recklessness in, or withdrawal from, international affairs, and was even able to take initiatives, when he was convinced of their necessity.

4

The Eisenhower Presidency
and foreign policy issues

The purpose of this chapter is to trace the influence of Eisenhower's conceptions of his role and of the office of the Presidency on some issues of American foreign policy during the 1950's.

In the previous chapter a comparison was made between Eisenhower's and Kennedy's concepts of the institutionalised Presidency, and we could reasonably conclude that their influence on policy-making was determined by the level at which they entered the process. In other words, it would be fair to assume than an active President who deals directly with experts in the various aspects of any issue would be in a better position to ensure that the decision which resulted reflected his own views, rather than one who is concerned to make the final decision only after a host of conflicting opinions have been reconciled. It is not surprising therefore that we should find, most readily, evidence of Eisenhower's influence on American foreign policy which is of a restraining rather than an active nature.

The new strategic policy

We need to consider first the Eisenhower Administration's defence strategy and its relationship to foreign policy. How did it reflect Eisenhower's own views and understanding, in addition to those of the orthodox, economy-minded conservatives who held important posts in his Administration? Secondly, we need to consider the extent to which the diplomatic implications of this policy, as they were carried out by the Secretary of State, reflected what would nowadays be termed Dulles' more 'hawk-like' attitude towards the Communist world, as opposed to Eisenhower's more 'dove-like' views.

The Eisenhower Administration, no less than its Democratic predecessor, was inclined to stress the military components of the power struggle between the United States and the Communist world. However, as opposed to the view that the United States economy could afford a continued high level of defence spending to the extent envisaged by the expansionist economists in the Truman Administration, the Republicans were convinced that such a course would lead to the ruin of the United States just as surely as if it were to be defeated in war by the Communists. The men who held major posts in the Eisenhower Administration were staunch economic conservatives and, as we have seen, there was little in the President's statements of his economic views to suggest that he, any less than they, held firmly to the homely virtues of thrift and solvency.

The Truman Administration had prepared a National Security Council paper (N.S.C.—141) for its successor which not only forecast a continued high level of military expenditure in the post-Korean War period, but actually proposed that it be increased. Eisenhower's reaction to this paper was that it ignored the connection between national security and fiscal responsibility. Nevertheless, if many of Eisenhower's Cabinet were Taft Republicans, the President himself was not willing to adopt the extreme position of Senator Taft and put tax-reductions and the balanced Budget ahead of national security requirements, as he understood them. Herein lay Eisenhower's problem. By April, 1953 he was able to announce a cut in new appropriations in the military budget of $7 billion. However, this was clearly little more than a gesture aimed at pacifying Taft and his supporters, and effected largely by not letting any new defence contracts for 1954. Real reductions or even a levelling off in defence expenditure demanded new concepts to replace those inherited from the previous Administration.

The Truman Administration had aimed its planning at a selected crisis year—1954—when it was said that the Soviet Union would be most capable of and likely to attack the West. Such a concept would tend to result in the creation of huge stock-piles of what would quickly become technologically obsolete weapons. Eisenhower therefore introduced a new plan, the 'long haul', which emphasised the creation of an industrial-technological base capable of supporting expanded production schedules whenever needed. Furthermore, by removing the crisis-year element, the 'long haul' also removed the sense of urgency under-lying the existing levels of defence expenditure, not only in the United States, but also in N.A.T.O. There it was very well received, and was indeed only formal recognition of a slackening which was already taking place.

In preparing his first Budget, the President ordered two major studies. The first was to explore a number of political-strategic policies, including the containment policy of the previous Administration, a deterrence policy with the threat of nuclear punishment, and a policy directed at the 'liberation' of Communist-held areas through economic, para-military and psychological warfare methods. The second study, undertaken by the newly selected Joint Chiefs of Staff, was charged with estimating the country's defence needs down to 1957. The results of this latter study were to reveal general agreement amongst the Joint Chiefs that U.S. military forces were over-extended and that for future conflicts in such potentially threatened areas—as, for example, Korea and Germany—prime responsibility should be undertaken by indigenous forces backed by American sea and air power. This would leave the American forces with the main task of protecting the continental United States and maintaining a massive retaliatory capability. However, none of the Joint Chiefs could see how their respective programmes could be cut, and when the military budget estimates for 1955 were presented to the National Security Council, the Secretary of the Treasury and the Director of the Budget in particular expressed profound disappointment that they had failed to provide for any significant reductions. The reaction of the Joint Chiefs was to insist that the only way substantially to reduce expenditure was for the Administration to take a basic policy decision on the kind of future war it envisaged. If the military could be assured that they would be allowed to use nuclear weapons whenever it was militarily advantageous to do so, then substantial savings could be made, since the doctrine then prevailing required the simultaneous maintenance of forces for brush-fire and limited conventional wars, conventional wars such as World War II, limited nuclear war, general nuclear war and any combination of these.

It appears that this argument had a profound impact on the Cabinet and on the President himself. By October 1953 general agreement had been reached within the Administration on the premises upon which its defence policy was to be based. These were spelt out first in National Security Council paper N.S.C.-162/2, in which it was stated that the military could count on using nuclear weapons, tactical and strategic, when militarily required. Force levels and deployment were to be planned on the basis that the fundamental objective of national security was to deter Soviet aggression—primarily by means of the massive retaliatory capability of the United States. In order to counter local aggressions, greater reliance would be placed on indigenous allied forces. As these were built up, American ground forces would eventually be reduced and any American participation in local actions would be mainly through tactical sea and air power and quickly-deployable mobile ground units, presumably using tactical nuclear weapons.

On the basis of these assumptions, the Joint Chiefs were

able to recommend a force posture, beginning with the 1955 Budget and maturing by 1957, which would result in a 25% drop in military manpower and a reduction of about $15 billion, from $50 to $35 billion, a year in defence expenditure.

It would seem from this analysis that there were essential differences between the defence policies of the Truman and Eisenhower Administrations which arose largely from their different economic philosophies. Indeed, most critics of the Eisenhower policy, while disagreeing on the virtues or otherwise of particular elements, all seem to agree that its sole rationale was the desire to reduce government expenditure even if it meant a loss of American bargaining power *vis-à-vis* the Soviet Union and a consequent risk to national security.

Another widespread criticism resulted largely from the manner in which Dulles presented the new policy to the world. For in first describing it Dulles scarcely mentioned the intention to place greater reliance on indigenous forces to deal with local conflicts. Instead, he stressed the heavy reliance to be placed in future on the massive capacity of the United States 'to retaliate instantly, by means and at places of our own choosing' (Dulles, 1954). Dulles was understood to be saying that the massive retaliatory capacity was to be the primary means of defence, not only for the continental United States, but for the entire Free World, thus narrowing down the possible choices of any threatened country to either accepting defeat or turning any local conflict into a major nuclear war. The fact that this was not the policy the Administration had in mind subsequently required a great deal of explanation on the part of Eisenhower, Dulles himself and other members of the Administration. Instead, they argued, it was their intention that local defence forces would still be important in denying the enemy easy territorial gains; that these local forces could be reinforced quickly by the central mobile reserve in the United States; and, finally, that the Communist powers would know that they could count on drawing the United States into a purely local encounter limited to the use of conventional weapons: the point being that the United States would be able to decide when and where to respond with its nuclear power.

For it does not seem likely that so far as Eisenhower was concerned economic considerations alone made him favour such a course. He was able to play a prominent part in the Truman defence establishment at a time when it had decisively abandoned economic stringency. Moreover, as a soldier himself it was unlikely that he would have tolerated any policy which he thought would have seriously jeopardised the national security of the United States, or go against its internationalist orientation. Other factors were involved. There was the President's clear determination to avoid as far as possible future American involvement in local wars of the type and extent of the Korean conflict. On the one hand, he believed that these were merely traps set by the Communists to drain American resources and weaken her for the main contest in Europe; on the other, he was concerned that the United States should not inherit the mantle of the old colonialist powers. His attitude towards Asian issues, such as Indochina and Taiwan, illustrates his first concern; his attitude towards the Middle East, particularly at the time of the Suez crisis, reflects the latter. There was, moreover, his concern to fulfil on the international scene the role he believed he had been called upon to play at home—namely, to bring unity and peace to a divided, antagonistic world.

Thus conservative economic theories were operationalised in the fields of foreign affairs and defence by the massive retaliation policy and its diplomatic implications. However, we can best see the influence of Eisenhower's conception of his role and of the office of the Presidency on American foreign policy during the 1950's if we consider the policy against the background of other factors that influenced the President's outlook.

Dulles and his relationship with Eisenhower

In so far as the new strategic policy stressed the role of indigenous military forces, it was Dulles' task, and, indeed, his major interest, to create and sustain the alliance structure to support this strategy.

John Foster Dulles' entire life down to November 1952 seems to have been spent in preparation for the Secretaryship of State. Dulles' grandfather, John Watson Foster, had served as Secretary of State between 1892 and 1893, and his uncle, Robert Lansing, had been Woodrow Wilson's Secretary of State at the time of the Versailles Peace Conference. At the age of nineteen, while a student at Princeton, Dulles accompanied his grandfather to the 1907 Hague Peace Conference, where he helped the Chinese delegation with protocol and translations. Having earned himself a reputation as a brilliant young lawyer, he attended the Versailles Conference as legal counsel to the American delegation on the Commission on Reparations. In 1944 he served as Foreign Policy Adviser to the Republican Presidential candidate, Thomas Dewey; subsequently, as a consultant to the State Department, he played a leading role in the negotiation and drafting of the Japanese Peace Treaty. He accepted commissions from the wartime and postwar Democratic Administrations largely because, through his association with Dewey, he had become a supporter of the bi-partisan foreign policy of which Senator Vandenberg was the leading Republican exponent.

Eisenhower, it has often been pointed out, was extremely impressed with Dulles' diplomatic credentials, and he regarded him as an expert in diplomacy whose professional expertise was to be respected in much the same way as he respected the military professionals on his staff during World War II and at N.A.T.O. Indeed, like Sherman Adams in the domestic sphere, the usual impression is that Dulles dominated American foreign policy during the Eisenhower Presidency. However, again like Sherman Adams, it seems that while the Secretary of State dominated the conduct of policy before his death, i.e. he was responsible for its style and execution, some reservations are necessary in attributing to him sole responsibility for the formation of policy.

It is more important to realise that Dulles remained Secretary of State for as long as he lived principally because, although there were differences between the attitudes of Eisenhower and himself towards certain aspects of foreign policy, Dulles was determined always to conform to Eisenhower's wishes. He was determined not to repeat the mistake of his uncle, Robert Lansing, who lost the confidence of Woodrow Wilson by pursuing an independent course while the latter was incapacitated. Thus if Dulles appeared over-concerned to conciliate the extremist Republican elements in Congress, then this clearly conformed to Eisenhower's conception of Executive-Congresssional relations. According to one of Dulles' biographers, at his first Cabinet meeting Eisenhower directed that there should be 100% co-operation with Congress, including McCarthy (Beal, 1959). Eisenhower would not quarrel with the Senator, and therefore Dulles' attitude was determined accordingly.

It had been Dulles' task to prepare the Republican foreign policy platform for the 1952 election campaign, a task which involved devising a policy statement that would not only contribute to winning the election, but would also reconcile all the different views within the Party, from the internationalists to the isolationists, and including also the McCarthyites. Despite Eisenhower's and his own connection with the previous Democratic government, Dulles solved his problem by launching an all-out attack on its policies. He accused the Democrats of having 'lost the peace so dearly earned in World War II', of having 'required the National Government of China to surrender Manchuria', and thus 'substituted on our Pacific flank a murderous enemy for an ally and friend', of having allowed 'more than five million non-Russian people of fifteen different countries to be absorbed into the power-sphere of Communist Russia', and of having brought 'on the Korean War through lack of foresight' (Bell, 1962, i. 70).

These statements contrasted strongly with Dulles' previous assessment of the Democratic policies. In 1949, for example, he had said: 'Soviet Communist tactics cannot prevail against such curative and creative programmes as we have been evolving over the past two years.' On the subject of Korea, he had been virtually unrestrained in his praise of Truman's decision to intervene. On as late as 19th May 1952 he wrote in *Life* magazine that 'President Truman's decision that the United States should go to the defence of the Korean Republic was courageous, righteous, and in the national interest'. In the same article he wrote: 'I can testify from personal knowledge that the President and Secretary of State [Dean Acheson] really want bi-partisanship and Congressional co-operation in foreign policy.' This was completely contradicted only a few weeks later when he insisted, in the Republican platform, that the G.O.P. had been ignored and not asked to participate in the foreign policy-making process.

When asked about these contradictions by Richard Rovere during the 1952 Republican Convention in Chicago, Dulles replied that as an individual he could not subscribe to some of the views expressed in the Republican policy statement, but that as a platform writer he was merely stating the Republican case against the Democratic Party (Rovere, 1956). Cynical as this statement clearly sounds, it nevertheless characterises what seems to be the essential Dulles. Trained as a lawyer, he was forever presenting a brief on behalf of a client, so that when he became Secretary of State, the United States became his client. His relations with Eisenhower seem to have been of a similar nature. R. Goold-Adams describes them as 'those of a good lawyer to a very old family friend who is also his client . . . he saw himself, on the one hand, briefing the President and, on the other, speaking for the President to the outside world' (Goold-Adams, 1962, i. 69). Thus, Eisenhower himself could write of his relationship with Dulles that it enabled him 'with complete confidence, to delegate to him an unusual degree of flexibility as my representative in international conferences, well knowing that he would not in the slightest degree operate outside the limits previously agreed between us' (Eisenhower, II, 1966, i. 365). The point about their relationship, however, was that it rarely operated so as to restrict Eisenhower when he wanted either to veto a certain course of action or pursue a somewhat different policy from that which Dulles was urging.

Eisenhower's outlook on foreign policy was more benign than that of Dulles, possibly because of their different experiences in the past and, to some extent, their general philosophical views. It is probably true to say that whereas Dulles tended to view the power struggle between the two super-powers and their allies as being one in which any gain for one side was a clear loss to the other, Eisenhower's experience and general conciliatory outlook on life led him to believe that differences could be resolved with some gain to both sides. For example, Dulles was initially opposed to the Geneva Summit Meeting of 1955 (Eisenhower, I, 1963). In late 1954 he reportedly told Mendès-France that he did not believe in the possibility of sincere constructive accords with Moscow as long as the Soviet Government was motivated by the treacherous doctrines of Leninism (Drummond & Coblentz, 1961). Eisenhower, on the other hand, had already said, on as early as 25th February 1953, that he would be prepared to meet Stalin halfway on the condition that the nation's allies were fully informed on the issues under discussion (Rostow, 1960).

Deference to domestic opinion

In examining the conduct of American foreign policy under Eisenhower, it is clear that one of its most striking aspects lay in its often excessively cautious regard for domestic opinion. This attitude was one which both Eisenhower and Dulles shared, although both were prepared to resist rather than reconcile opinion when it seemed likely to jeopardise basic policy positions. Nevertheless, the Administration was markedly circumspect in its dealings with Senator McCarthy.

The Eisenhower Administration took office when McCarthy was at the height of his influence as Chairman of the Senate's Permanent Sub-committee on Investigations. In the early months of 1953 McCarthy was successful in securing the appointment by Dulles of one of the Senator's leading supporters, Scott McCleod, as security officer in the State Department in order to purge it of the Communists. Having condemned the appointment of James B. Conant, President of Harvard University, as High Commissioner for Germany, the Senator and his supporters challenged the assignment of Charles E. Bohlen as Ambassador to the Soviet Union, denouncing him as Acheson's architect of disaster. Bohlen's only crime, as it was subsequently proved when his appointment was confirmed through the influence of Senator Taft, was to have served under the two previous Democratic Administrations and to have been present at the Yalta Conference.

Another manifestation of McCarthyism to which Eisenhower reacted with some degree of diffidence was the infamous book-burning episode. On 19th February 1953 the State Department's Information Agency attempted to pacify McCarthy by banning the use by overseas missions of any material written by suspected Communists or fellow-travellers. Since the Secretary of State's directives never clearly defined which books and which authors were to be excluded, officials overseas removed from their libraries magazines and books, some of which were burned, that were never to appear on any list of unacceptable publications—all this without really satisfying the Senator.

Shortly after this episode McCarthy began to attack the Administration's foreign policy directly, denouncing the continuation of the mutual assistance programme with Britain while the latter traded with Communist China. A curious, yet related, incident was the 'agreement' reached between McCarthy and a group of Greek shipowners to the effect that they would order their vessels to cease trading with the Communist Chinese. This produced a strong protest from Harold Stassen, Eisenhower's Director of Mutual Security, who argued that McCarthy was undermining American foreign policy. Eisenhower himself refused to become involved directly, and when, at a subsequent Press conference, he was questioned by reporters on the affair, he refused to even criticise the Senator by name, making his now famous statement, 'I will not get into the gutter with that guy' (*Presidential Papers*, 1953).

The Greek shipping episode was settled amicably at a lunch between McCarthy and Dulles. Eisenhower and his Secretary of State were obliged to defend their conduct of Anglo-American relations more forcefully, and decisively rejected the idea that the United States could coerce her Allies and deal with them in any way except as sovereign equals. On the whole, however, McCarthyism did untold damage to American prestige abroad, particularly when the Senator's lieutenants, Cohn and Schine, began investigating American missions in Europe. Moreover, it is likely that the damage was compounded by Eisenhower's refusal to take any vigorous action against the Senator.

In addition to the McCarthy issue, Eisenhower faced another major challenge from Congress early in his Administration in the form of the so-called Bricker Amendment. Ostensibly the purpose of the Amendment was to provide protection against the possibility that any President, aided by an apathetic Senate, would enter into treaty obligations which would deprive the American people of their constitutional rights or would infringe the powers of the separate states to conduct their own internal affairs. As it was eventually presented to the Congress in March 1953, Senator Bricker's resolution contained two provisions: one was designed to regulate all Executive and other agreements; the other to prevent the President and Senate from making treaties which were likely in any way to affect internal or domestic matters as opposed to purely international concerns. In fact, the first provision was aimed principally against such Executive agreements as that entered into at Yalta in early 1945 by the Roosevelt Administration. It was believed that the Yalta Agreement (which was never fully published) contained important concessions to the Soviet Union which had been wrung out of the ailing President with the help of the Communists and subversives who had infiltrated his staff. The second provision was designed to forestall acceptance of treaties drafted by the United Nations and its agencies. It was felt that such treaties would force the individual states of the Union to accept domestic reforms against their wishes and thereby infringe such constitutional autonomy as they possessed in these matters. Above all, however, it became quite clear to Eisenhower and his colleagues that, if it were passed, the Bricker Amendment would considerably reduce the powers of the Presidency to conduct foreign relations.

Senator Bricker's proposals aroused tremendous controversy in the country and presented a dual problem to Eisenhower himself. Very early on he was persuaded that he needed to hold on firmly to his powers in the field of foreign affairs. Nevertheless, he was not by inclination unsympathetic to those who believed that the Executive had become too powerful at the expense of the other branches of government. Moreover, the main impetus for the constitutional changes came from members of his own Party in the Senate. Extended discussions took place between the Administration and Bricker and his supporters, in the hope that some agreement could be reached to satisfy both sides. When this proved impossible, there was nothing left to do 'but get ready for a fight to the end' (Eisenhower, I, i. 283). Critics have often argued that the controversy over the Bricker Amendment illustrated a basic failing in Eisenhower's approach to the Presidency and his view of Executive-Congressional relations. They have argued that there could be no relationship based on conciliation and compromise when the Congress was set upon detracting from the powers of the President and augmenting its own. Any other modern President, it is said, would have attempted from the outset to exercise strong leadership, both in order to operate effectively and to get his programmes through Congress. From the point of view of this study, however, it would be wrong to have expected Eisenhower to hold such a view. He was a Republican and a conservative, with an appropriately conservative view of the Constitution. If he was eventually forced to fight, then this was because he was convinced that his position was constitutionally correct.

Moreover, at that time he felt strongly, like most Presidents, the need to unite his party behind him and certainly to have a friendly rather than hostile Congress. Eisenhower's difficulties in this respect were described at the end of the previous chapter. The experience of his strong successors, Kennedy and Johnson, has since shown that they were not very much more successful than he in dealing with Congress, even when it contained majorities of their own supporters.

Far-Eastern policy

The Administration's Asian policy illustrated Eisenhower's determination not to be drawn into local wars if they could be avoided, and also to resist the extremists in Congress when they attempted to influence his basic policy position.

Eisenhower did not allow the powerful 'Asia first' faction in Congress, whose membership included at that time Senators Taft and Knowland, in addition to McCarthy and Jenner, to stand in the way of a settlement of the Korean War. He regarded their demands to enlarge the conflict into a great sea and air offensive along the lines suggested by General MacArthur as completely unfeasible. At a Press conference he disagreed with Senator Taft, who argued that if the stalemate in the negotiations continued the nation should 'go it alone'. He declared that he had no intention of abandoning the system of collective security to which the country was committed. 'If you are going to go it alone one place,' he said, 'you . . . have to go it alone everywhere . . .' (*Presidential Papers*, 1953, i. 329).

A settlement was eventually achieved in Korea in July 1953 along the lines developed during the Truman Administration. Eisenhower had fulfilled one of his principal campaign pledges, and in so doing incurred the odium only of the extreme right wing of his own party, who denounced the settlement as a peace without honour.

The Indochina crisis of 1954 is one of the clearest examples of Eisenhower's concern to avoid American involvement in another Korean-type conflict. The decision not to intervene on behalf of the beleaguered French garrison at Dienbienphu does not seem to be merely illustrative of the poverty of the Administration's strategic policy as some commentators believe it to have been. Rather it seems to reflect the basic policy position that in such areas the United States would not intervene alone without allies and without the existence of adequate indigenous forces to take a major share of the burden. Dulles, having failed to persuade the Allies, and particularly Britain, to take common action, was apparently ready for the Americans to go it alone out of the conviction that a Communist victory would have serious repercussions for American interests in the Far East as a whole. Eisenhower, according to General Mathew B. Ridgeway, overruled not only Dulles, but also the Chairman of the Joint Chiefs of Staff, Admiral Radford. The decision not to intervene was due only partly to the British refusal to participate. Principally it was because Eisenhower accepted the report of an Army study which showed that even an air strike would inevitably have resulted in the commitment of ground forces at a cost in manpower and money as great, if not greater, than the Korean War.

To a man of his military experience [Ridgeway asserts] its [the report's] implications were immediately clear.

> The idea of intervening was abandoned, and it is my
> belief that the analysis which the army made . . . played
> a considerable, perhaps a decisive, part in persuading our
> government not to embark on the tragic adventure
> (Ridgeway, 1961, i. 119).

Indeed, Eisenhower himself, as he recounts in his memoirs,
told his advisers that if the United States were unilaterally
to permit its forces to be drawn into conflict in Indochina
and in a succession of Asian wars, the end-result would be
to drain off American resources and weaken her overall
defensive position (Eisenhower, I, 1963).

During this period Eisenhower also successfully resisted
efforts by Republican leaders in Congress to rigidify even
further American policy towards China. Early on in his
term of office, he ignored an appeal by Senator Jenner that
he issue a final statement that the United States would not
recognise the Peking Government or consent to its admis-
sion to the United Nations under any circumstances (Warren, 1964). He also opposed a rider to an appropriations
Bill, introduced by Republican Senator Everett Dirksen,
under which American contributions to the United Nations
budget would be terminated automatically if Communist
China was admitted to membership (Donovan, 1956). Indeed, until mid-1955 Eisenhower was under constant pressure from his military advisers, Senators, and, in the case
of Indochina, even from Dulles, to pursue a more aggressive, adventurous policy in the Far East. Instead, a much
more moderate policy was followed, for Eisenhower, in
effect, made few concessions to the so-called China lobby,
and certainly no more than was made by President Truman.

During the first few days of the Korean War, President
Truman ordered the U.S. Seventh Fleet to be stationed in
the straits between Formosa and the Chinese mainland,
both to prevent Communist attacks on the island and
forays by the Nationalists against the mainland. Truman
was concerned not to allow the Communists an excuse for
reprisal action that would widen the area of conflict
(Truman, Vol. II, 1965).

Considerable alarm was caused in both the United Kingdom and France when, in his first State of the Union Message, President Eisenhower announced that the Seventh Fleet would no longer be employed to shield Communist China. Yet the so-called 'unleashing' of Chiang Kai-shek was important mainly for American domestic politics: to show the determination of the new Administration to get tough with the Communists, as well as being part of an intensive effort to end the Korean War by any means. Its long-term diplomatic consequences, as an additional factor in exacerbating American relations with the Chinese Communists, were of no little importance, yet militarily it was a meaningless act. For whether the American Seventh Fleet prevented Chiang from attacking the mainland or not, the truth was that, without large-scale direct American help, he was securely leashed by his own lack of strength. Under Eisenhower, Chiang was given more American military aid than before, but not very much more.

The Eisenhower Presidency, down until mid-1955, achieved by virtue of the President's conduct of his office a number of things for which he is generally given too little credit. He did not succeed in bringing all Americans around to his view of foreign policy, but he did essentially create an atmosphere in which the opinions of men like Senators Bridges, Knowland and McCarthy, which were really more representative of Republican thought than his own, were looked upon as deviationist in character. Moreover, he succeeded in bringing American opinion generally to accept a far more sophisticated view of the world. Whereas, when he took office, Americans still thought in terms of once-for-all solutions to problems in international relations, by 1955 they were reconciled to his concept of the 'long haul', not only in terms of military expenditure, but in regard to the entire strategic-political position of the United States in the world.

Peace initiatives

Simultaneously with his efforts to reconcile public opinion and, hopefully, the Republican Party to his moderate views on foreign policy, Eisenhower's personal influence can also be traced in the United States' early attempts to reach an understanding with the Soviet Union, with a view to negotiating, if not a settlement of the Cold War issues, then at least a mitigation of the mounting arms race. Three elements appear to have converged in making Eisenhower look favourably on the prospects for negotiations, two of them derived from his military experience.

The first was his service on the Control Council in Berlin during 1945-6. Eisenhower, in common with many other Americans who came into contact with the modern Soviet soldiers and technicians at that time, was left with the impression that they exhibited values and manners quite different from what had been expected. In particular, the Americans felt that, given time, Soviet society might evolve into something different from what it appeared to be under Stalin, one with which coexistence might be possible.

Secondly, Eisenhower's military experience left him with a realistic appreciation of the far greater destructive potential of nuclear weapons, as compared with the weapons of World War II, and this made him regard major war as not only irrational, but unthinkable. For example, in a speech to a group of State Department officials in October 1954, he said, 'since the advent of nuclear weapons, it seems clear that there is no longer any alternative to peace', and on the following day at a college in Hartford (Conn.) he added, 'war would present to us only the alternatives in degrees of destruction' (Rovere, 1956, i. 235). At any event, Eisenhower seems to have believed that the United States would have to look to non-military instruments to protect its interests, and this was reflected very early on in the appointment in his Cabinet of a Special Assistant in charge of Cold War psychology planning.

The third factor consisted of the commitment of the

Eisenhower Administration to seek a substantial reduction in defence expenditure, an issue which has already been discussed in some detail above.

Eisenhower's address to the American Society of Newspaper Editors of 16th April 1953, 'The Chance for Peace', represented his response to the death of Stalin some six weeks previously, and defined some of his thinking and intentions on peaceful relations without any specific commitment to negotiate. He did, however, list a number of issues for negotiation, including Korea, Indochina, Austria, Germany and the international control of armaments. In respect of the last issue, Eisenhower went out of his way to convey to the new Soviet leaders his appreciation of the mutual benefits to be derived from substantial disarmament:

> Every gun that is made, every warship launched, every rocket fired signifies in the final sense, a theft from those who hunger and are not fed, those who are cold and are not clothed (Eisenhower, I, 1963, i. 145).

In addition, Eisenhower's concern about the consequences of nuclear war, particularly after the detonation of the Soviet H-bomb in August 1953, led in the December of that year to his 'Atoms for Peace' proposal. As he recounts it, the idea occurred to the President that the United States and the Soviet Union could each donate fissionable material to the United Nations which could be devoted to peaceful projects under international supervision (Eisenhower, I, 1963).

These peace moves, together with the initiative to go to the Summit Meeting in Geneva in 1955, belonged to Eisenhower himself, and did not involve, in any essential way, his Secretary of State. The 'Chance for Peace' address was devised principally with the aid of his White House staff, and was drafted by his chief speech-writer at that time, Emmet Hughes. The 'Atoms for Peace' proposal was worked out by Special Assistants Robert Cutler and C. D. Jackson and the Chairman of the Atomic Energy Commission,

Admiral Louis Strauss. As Sherman Adams put it, 'an idealistic venture like the "Atoms for Peace" plan was hardly the sort of thing that would fire the imagination of a man like Dulles' (Brown, 1968, i. 91).

There was obviously some considerable lack of realism in these proposals, largely because there was little likelihood of the Soviet Union agreeing to them. A further initiative, Eisenhower's 'Open Spies' plan for the mutual aerial inspection of disarmament, which he presented at the Geneva Summit Conference, was equally doomed to a sceptical reception. Moreover, like many of Eisenhower's initiatives, they tended to be dissipated through the processes of his governmental machine.

There was (as was explained in Chapter 3) the lack of an intermediary between himself and Dulles, and indeed other members of his Administration concerned with foreign affairs. Their constant demands on the President's time meant that he was concerned excessively with the problems of day-to-day diplomacy. Thus Emmet Hughes reports that Eisenhower's 'Chance for Peace' address was not followed by a vigorous effort to negotiate with the Soviet Union because he was too involved at that time with current problems, such as the futile campaign to induce the French to ratify the European Defence Community Pact (Hughes, 1963).

It is here then, that we reach the heart of Eisenhower's dilemma. President Truman's famous prophecy about Eisenhower's problems as President is relevant. ' "He'll sit here," Truman would say, "and he'll say, 'Do this! Do that!' *And nothing will happen*. Poor Ike—it won't be a bit like the Army. He'll find it very frustrating" ' (*Neustadt*, 1964, i. 22). Neustadt reports that Eisenhower suffered such 'frustration' even as late as 1958, when one of his aides remarked : 'The President still feels that when he's decided something, that ought to be the end of it . . . and when it bounces back undone or done wrong he tends to react with shocked surprise' (*Neustadt*, 1964, i 22).

During his first term of office, however, Eisenhower

58

conceived of his role as being to reconcile American domestic opinion. He was, as already stated, determined to end the Korean War, to take some of the acrimony out of the American political atmosphere, and to restore and maintain fiscal prudence. In this he was as successful as any Republican President could have been. He was continually praised during 1956, and Richard Rovere, a sceptical critic in 1953, could write of his performance in foreign affairs in the most glowing terms. 'Eisenhower,' Rovere said, 'attempted to meet . . . [his] . . . responsibilities in a spirit of decency and maturity that has been a credit to him and to the country' (Rovere, 1956, i. 373).

Alternative instruments of power

One of the major problems facing any government in respect of foreign affairs is the difficulty in recognising changes in the international environment and then adjusting its policies to take account of them. Until 1955-6 the Eisenhower Administration held to its view of a bi-polar world, of the international situation as a struggle between two competing monolithic power blocs, seeing any conflict, anywhere in the world, as part of the global struggle between the Communists and the Free World. The Suez and Hungarian crises, which happened by chance to coincide in 1956, dramatised certain fissiparous tendencies within the two blocs and, perhaps more importantly, they illustrated the failings of relying too exclusively on the military instruments of power. In the Middle East, for example, the purpose of the American government was to counter the growing Soviet influence and compensate for the failure of the Western Alliance in that area (through the Baghdad Pact), to prevent this. The purpose of the British and French governments was to ensure their supplies of oil and to regain their hold over the Suez Canal. These aims were not incompatible, but there were great differences between the means the allies chose to employ to secure them. The President's personal views, together

59

with the overall concern of his Administration to maintain the global balance of power, led the Americans to seek to demonstrate their respect for Arab nationalism and seek to make it more favourable to the West.

The fact was that the Eisenhower Administration did begin to move from concentrating mainly on the military components of the power balance to a more sophisticated view of the requirements for maintaining the balance. However, a more coherent and deliberate policy in this respect did not emerge until Eisenhower had left office, and has still not matured, as the American involvement in the Vietnam War has shown.

Eisenhower's peace initiatives, his 'Open Skies' proposal at the Geneva Summit Conference included, all appear to have indicated that he was not himself insensitive to the potential effectiveness of alternative methods of diplomacy to the purely military instruments that were being emphasised by his Administration. However, it was not until the Czech-Egyptian arms deal of 1955 highlighted the effectiveness of Soviet aid policies in leapfrogging the American alliance structure and penetrating areas of such strategic importance as the Middle East that the views of the Eisenhower Administration towards foreign aid began to be revised.

Up until this episode foreign aid tended to be regarded strictly within the context of winning and supporting allies who agreed to join the American alliance structure in the bi-polar struggle. The relationship between economic development, social reform and resistance to Communist subversion was yet to be seen as having any bearing on the means of securing a favourable international environment.

Nevertheless, the offer and subsequent withdrawal of financial assistance to the Egyptians in constructing the Aswan Dam, while a major factor in precipitating the Suez Crisis at the end of 1956, can be seen as the first, albeit unsophisticated, move in the American adjustment to this view. The withdrawal of the offer of the loan is seen by most commentators as the critical step towards the eventual crisis. It certainly precipitated the nationalisation of the Canal and the consequent reactions of the British and French governments. However, it was the manner and timing of the withdrawal that has been criticised most severely, more so than the actual withdrawal itself. It was a sudden, dramatic move by Dulles the lawyer, tactlessly administered as a deliberate rebuff to President Nasser when he was visiting Marshal Tito at Brioni. Yet if the manner of the withdrawal has been generally condemned, even by Eisenhower himself, the substance of the decision certainly enjoyed more widespread approval. It was true that within the Administration, the President, Vice-President and to some extent the Secretary of State, among others, were tentatively exploring a new approach to their dealings with the emerging nationalism in the underdeveloped areas. In the Congress, on the other hand, there was even less willingness then than there is now to accept the idea of economic competition with the Communists for influence in the Third World. At that time the Administration was sensitive both to the opposition of the Congress to foreign aid and to the critical climate towards neutralism then prevalent in Washington. As the President and Dulles became convinced that the Egyptians were playing them off against the Russians in an effort to secure more favourable terms, the cancellation of the offer was always likely.

Suez again illustrated Eisenhower's general unwillingness to be drawn into a conflict which could well lead to a direct confrontation with the Soviet Union or at the very least to the direct association of the United States with the old colonial powers in the eyes of the non-aligned countries. This seemed to hold even when the ex-colonial powers were important allies, such as Britain and France. Despite Eden's statements to the contrary, Eisenhower's position was clear from the time he first learned that Britain and France were seriously planning a military action. In his negotiations with the allies, Dulles operated under strict instructions from the President that he was to prevent military intervention on their part, otherwise they would forfeit the support of the United States.

It was not until 1958 that a series of crises, again in the Middle East, finally resulted in the announcement of a policy which sought to stabilise socio-economic conditions in an underdeveloped area, regardless of the existence of neutralist or even overt anti-Western sentiments in the region. This new approach was contained in Eisenhower's address to the United Nation's General Assembly on 13th August 1958. The President proposed a regional develop-ment plan for the Middle East which was analogous to the Marshall Plan in early postwar Europe. He pledged United States financial support for a development programme to be formulated and managed by the Arab nations them-selves.

Just as the strategic policy of the Eisenhower Administra-tion ruled out intervention in local wars in the so-called Third World, the failure of the United States to intervene in the Hungarian uprising was a decisive demonstration that it would not become involved in similar actions in eastern Europe. The run-down of conventional forces meant that the United States lacked the means to intervene in an area where the Soviet Union had overwhelming superiority in such forces.

Hungary was also a final convincing demonstration that the part of the 1952 Republican Party platform which called for the liberation of Communist-controlled countries in Eastern Europe was little more than campaign rhetoric. Indeed, it had no place in the Administration's new strategic policy, although it was considered by one of the study groups mentioned above. However, the break-up of the Soviet bloc, which events in Hungary and Poland revealed, showed that it was possible to enter into economic rela-tions with the European satellites along the lines of those already established with the Tito Government in Yugo-slavia. The tendency at least to experiment with such relations in the aftermath of the Hungarian crisis fitted in with Eisenhower's general view of his role during his second term of office.

Eisenhower's second term

During his second term, Eisenhower devoted increasing attention to foreign affairs, and specifically to the problems of reaching some agreement with the Soviet Union on the issues of world peace, paying less attention to the questions of day-to-day diplomacy. The picture is more of a President growing old in office, anticipating his retirement, but desperate to realise one overarching historic mission. This somewhat simple, romantic view of Eisenhower during his last years in office is, it seems, essential to an understanding of his outlook on world affairs at the time. He had to run for re-election in 1956, he told his friends, because 'I want to advance our chances for world peace, if only by a little maybe only a few feet' (Goldman, 1962, i. 327). In 1958 he stated at a Press conference: 'There is no place on this earth to which I would not travel, there is no chore I would not undertake, if I had any faintest hope that, by so doing, I would promote the general cause of world peace' (Goldman, 1962, i. 327). Nevertheless, he accepted Dulles' advice not to agree to another Summit in that year.

There seems, however, to have been some justification from the American point of view for rejecting a meeting at that time. Khrushchev's call for a Summit was preceded by his declaration that, unless a new arrangement on Berlin was negotiated within six months, he would sign a peace treaty with East Germany, implying that it would then have sovereign authority to deal with Berlin and control access to the city. The Americans at this particular time felt that they were in a somewhat inferior bargaining position *vis-à-vis* the Soviet Union, particularly in the light of what was then regarded as their unfavourable position in the nuclear strategic balance. Hence, it does not seem likely that Dulles was hard pressed to persuade Eisenhower to reject Khrushchev's call.

Moreover, there is equally reason for thinking that Eisenhower's agreement to a Summit after Dulles' death in 1959 was not due solely to his release from his 'gaoler'. Through-

63

out 1959 there was constant pressure for another Summit, both within the United States and abroad, particularly from Britain. Furthermore, the United States' rejection of the 1958 Summit was being exploited by Khrushchev as evidence of Soviet peaceful intentions and American intransigent hostility. Again, this period saw a number of scientific, cultural and social exchanges between the Soviet Union and the United States, culminating, in July 1959, in Vice-President Nixon's visit to Moscow. Finally, it seems, Eisenhower's objections to a further Summit were removed by Khrushchev's visit to the United States in September 1959.

The climax of the visit was the period the two leaders spent at Camp David, the President's retreat. If, at Geneva in 1955, Eisenhower was able to impress the Russians with his peaceful intentions, at Camp David Khrushchev seems to have made a similar impression on Eisenhower. At a subsequent Press conference Eisenhower told reporters that the conversations at Camp David had 'removed many of the objections that I have heretofore held to a Big Four meeting' (Goldman, 1962, i. 332). Specifically, this was understood to mean that Khrushchev had agreed to remove his ultimatum about Berlin.

The lame duck President

Eisenhower says of his 22,000-mile eleven-nation tour of December 1959 that he decided to carry it out because he felt that rather than spend the remainder of his Presidency marking time, waiting for 20th January 1961, suffering the decline in his influence which normally attends a President's last year in office, he decided to use his personal prestige and wide acquaintanceship to further United States diplomacy (Eisenhower, II, 1966). It seems, however, that his tour had a somewhat more specific purpose. The idea was for Eisenhower to fulfil the role in world affairs he was best suited for : to bring as much neutral opinion as possible behind the West and to smooth out differences among

64

the Western allies in preparation for a new Summit meeting. Eisenhower's tour was an all-round success, a tremendous exercise in public relations. His enthusiastic reception in India, in particular, was in strong contrast with that accorded to Vice-President Nixon in Caracas in 1958, and suggests that, not only in the United States, but also in the world at large, Eisenhower's personal popularity far exceeded that of his Administration. His efforts at reconciling De Gaulle to the idea of a Summit were more strenuous, but possibly no less successful, and the date for the meeting with Khrushchev was fixed for May 1960.

From the point of view of this study, it is appropriate enough that the last major diplomatic move of the Eisenhower Administration should have been the abortive Summit meeting of May 1960. For if anything, it illustrated at one and the same time the discrepancy between Eisenhower's willingness to negotiate with the Soviet Union and the problems of bad co-ordination and sluggish response of his Administration in the field of foreign affairs. The initial denial and then Eisenhower's assumption of personal responsibility for ordering the flight of the U.2 reconnaisance plane over the U.S.S.R. on the eve of the conference was indicative of this.

The disastrous U.2 incident however, was probably more the occasion for the Summit failure than its true cause. For it was not possible for Eisenhower to make any real concessions over Berlin and the German question. The position of Berlin, an enclave deep in East Germany, was —mistakenly, some thought—freely admitted by Eisenhower to be an anomaly. Not having sufficient conventional forces in Europe to counter a limited Soviet threat, the United States could only reply to any attack on Berlin by threatening major nuclear war. Such a threat was unlikely to impress the Soviet Union, who could not be expected to believe that the Americans would launch a total war in such conditions. It was left therefore to the incoming Democratic Administration, with its determination to redress the balance of conventional military capabilities in Europe, to continue to seek a solution to the German question.

The effects of Eisenhower's successors' views and conduct of American foreign policy are conceivably more easy to discern. But it is questionable whether they, very much more than he, have yet found it possible to discover a coherent foreign policy and of conducting it to the optimum effect.

5
Conclusion

Personalisation of foreign policy

One of the most notable features of any policy outcome, in domestic as well as in foreign affairs, is its tendency to become personalised. In the Press, radio and on television, in private discussion as well as in academic treatises, the practice is to use such terms as the 'Truman Doctrine', the 'Eisenhower Doctrine' and 'Johnson's Vietnam policy'. In many people's minds, the Cuban missile crisis of 1962 was thought of more as a contest between Kennedy and Khrushchev than as a confrontation between the governments of the two most powerful states in the world and their unimaginably complex bureaucracies.

In theory, if not in fact, the American Presidency is the most powerful political office in the world. The Constitution stipulates that the President is simultaneously Head of State, Chief Executive, Commander-in-Chief of the Armed Forces, Chief Diplomat and Chief Legislator. In modern times the President has acquired a number of extra-Constitutional functions in party leadership, in the management of the economy, in preserving the peace and, by means of his easy access to the mass media, in leading public opinion. Small wonder therefore that, particularly in the field of foreign policy, where the government has a virtual monopoly over the sources of information and in which often remote issues of great complexity are involved, policies should be personalised in the manner described above. For in a very real sense, even if it is only marginally involved in the policy-making process, the President is personally responsible for the outcome.

Yet there is another sense in which it is justifiable to describe, not only particular policies by the name of, say, the incumbent President, but the entire period of his office. For one of the main purposes of this study has been to show that, however difficult it is to isolate the President's personal influence on a particular foreign policy decision, even in the case of the most passive President, policy-making during his term of office is characterised by his view of his role and of his office and his general outlook on the world, or, in brief, by his style.

Eisenhower's style

Eisenhower has been described in this study as a passive President. Essentially he was a conservative who was not concerned with change, even in the field of foreign affairs, so much as consolidating changes that had already taken place. As the last chapter has shown, his initiatives were few and far between. Thus it is difficult to find signs of Eisenhower's own influence on many specific policy decisions.

Nevertheless, it is not necessary to go as far as W. W. Rostow in criticising Eisenhower for not imposing his own insights, his own sense of direction, on United States foreign policy during his term of office (Rostow, 1960). For although, as an innovator, Eisenhower was a passive President, he seems nearly always to have been able to ensure that United States policy as a whole conformed to the essential premises he had laid down, even if his institutional conception of the Presidency meant that he was unable to influence the conduct of policy in its particular aspects. For example, in his memoirs Eisenhower says that he subsequently regretted the abruptness of Dulles' action in withdrawing the offer of the Aswan Dam loan to the Egyptians (Eisenhower, II, 1966). While this is one of the

68

very rare occasions in his memoirs when Eisenhower mentions any substantial disagreement with the Secretary of State's actions, there were probably other such incidents which the President was unable to prevent.

Although we have listed the major functions and powers attributable to the President personally, it seems virtually impossible for any one man to exercise his powers fully in any one of these areas. Any President must delegate his powers to some extent, and it seems unreasonable to hold him to account for every action, failure or otherwise, throughout his administration.

This seems to have been Eisenhower's view of his office. His role was to select the ablest men, to delegate his powers as broadly as possible, and to see that the high policy lines he authorised should be adhered to as closely as possible. So far as he himself was concerned, he was to set a high personal example of honesty and goodwill: to stay above the political struggle, as free as possible from the entanglements of day-to-day administration, so that he could act as the focus of the national purpose. There was a considerable gulf between the aspirational and operational levels of this view. In respect of foreign affairs, his Administration was not the smoothly working machine he hoped it would be. However, on the aspirational level, we can see the essence of Eisenhower's style. He was largely able to maintain his own personal prestige throughout his Presidency, though his Administration was often heavily criticised.

The interdependency of domestic and foreign policy

In Chapter 4 of this study we abstracted for analytical purposes those issues during Eisenhower's Presidency in which it was possible to discern most clearly his attitudes and influence in foreign affairs. However, in foreign-policy analysis it is impossible to ignore the essential interdependency between domestic and foreign policy—indeed, between domestic politics and foreign policy-making. For neither of these operate in a vacuum and they cannot be separated. This holds true in the United States in particular, but it is probably the case anywhere in the world. Thus in order to explain how foreign-policy decisions are arrived at it is essential to understand the domestic political environment in which such policy is made. The chief policy-maker—in this case the President of the United States—is essentially sensitive to the domestic political situation, even if, like Eisenhower, he believes himself to be above politics.

Between 1932 and 1952 the Federal Government had grown to huge proportions. This had been due to events both at home and abroad : intervention on a massive scale to regulate the national economy and involvement in World War II and the subsequent Cold War. In order to meet these new responsibilities, countless government agencies were established and a huge bureaucracy had come into being. The President increased his powers considerably, particularly in the field of legislation. Presidents Roosevelt and Truman urged countless measures and Bills on a Congress which resented the encroachment of the Executive into what they regarded as legitimately belonging to their sphere of government.

Thus the Roosevelt era came to be regarded by many Americans, both in the Congress and throughout the United States, as a time of great crisis in domestic and international affairs, which required unorthodox crisis solutions. But by the time President Truman reached the end of his term of office it appeared that more than half the population desired a return to what they believed to be 'normality'. Indeed, they included many people who had benefited from the enhanced Federal Government activity, but who in their current situation deeply resented high taxation and all the other encroachments of 'big government' on their lives.

However, the nature of American society and economy and the postwar international environment meant that there could be no return to a free economy unhindered by government regulation, any more than it was possible

70

to retreat back into isolationism.

In Chapter 2 a brief account was given of the national mood in the United States when Eisenhower took office; McCarthyism and the Bricker Amendment were discussed in Chapter 4. McCarthy conducted an anti-Communist witch-hunt aimed principally at the State Department. Bricker, ostensibly anxious to preserve the rights of the separate states of the Union, aimed his attack at the Presidency. However, both achieved considerable prominence because they gave expression to the underlying resentment against the powerful Presidency and the huge centralised government machine that Roosevelt and Truman had left behind. Thus when a conservative career diplomat, Robert Murphy, was recalled from Japan in 1953 to take up a senior post at the State Department, he was asked by a friend, 'Bob, how can you bring yourself to work in that nest of Commies and homosexuals in the State Department?' (Murphy, 1964, i. 444). That question epitomised a popular attitude at the time towards the Federal establishment in general and the State Department in particular.

Throughout this study there has been continual emphasis on the fact that Eisenhower, as a conservative, was inclined to sympathise with the premises underlying this popular attitude. Furthermore, if he had any political acumen at all, he realised the need to conciliate opinion, especially in the Republican Party, on this issue above all others.

Eisenhower was a simple man. He had an unsophisticated view of politics, but it has been a major purpose of this study to show that he was not an innocent wandering through the complex morass of modern American political life. He had very definite views, and if his term of office was remarkable for its lack of strong Presidential leadership and initiatives, on the lines of his two immediate predecessors, then this was deliberate on his part. As Gore Vidal, who was distressed by Eisenhower's attitude, has put it :

> . . . Eisenhower's open disdain of politics and his con-
> viction that 'politician' was a dirty word . . . is shared
> . . . by the majority of the American electorate, ex-
> plaining the General's continuing appeal. Time and time
> again during those years one used to hear : 'O.K., so he
> is a lousy President, but thank God he isn't a politician'
> (Ions, 1967, i. 74).

Eisenhower's influence

During the last few years it has been very fashionable to
criticise the Eisenhower Presidency, and especially the
President's view of his role. However, he left his successor
a much more settled and united country, one which was
not unresponsive to President Kennedy's call for change,
and certainly prepared to accept a new approach to foreign
affairs. With the advent of the Kennedy Administration,
American foreign policy entered a new active phase.
Foreign-aid programmes became more commonly and
regularly acceptable as alternatives to the military components of power. The Foreign Assistance Act of 1961 and
the Alliance for Progress in Latin America were early
evidence of this new approach. It was possible, moreover,
for the Kennedy Administration to accept the neutralisa-
tion of Laos, to threaten intervention on behalf of forces
opposed to the dictatorship in the Dominican Republic and
to grant economic assistance to radical African nationalists,
such as Sekou Touré. It was also possible for Kennedy to
call off the Bay of Pigs intervention in Cuba and, following
the missile crisis of 1962, to sign the Nuclear Test-ban
Treaty as the prelude to a *détente* with the Soviet Union.

For it does seem possible to suggest that under Eisenhower America had time to mature and become reconciled
to a more sophisticated world role. Perhaps one of the
most interesting aspects of the Vietnam issue has been
the absence in political circles of witch-hunts, of blaming
America's problems on subversives and the machinations
of international Communism, as there were at the time
of Korea. Instead, Americans are blaming themselves.

Moreover, although he disapproved of 'big government', Eisenhower did not surrender any of the powers of the President, so that Kennedy could enter into the office and exercise as much power as his immediate Democratic predecessors. Furthermore, it is now too little appreciated that under Eisenhower the prestige of the Presidency was revived out of the disrepute into which the office had fallen during Truman's last years. This too made it easier for President Kennedy to influence public opinion in the direction he desired.

Currently American society is again divided, in part because of the problems of poverty and violence in the cities. However, the Vietnam issue is no less important a cause. The analysis undertaken in this study suggests, in respect of the latter issue, that President Eisenhower's conservative economic views, his understanding of the military implications of deep involvement in such a war, and, above all, his appreciation of the divisive influence it would be likely to have on American society, meant that he conceivably would have pursued a different policy from his successors.

To return to the original proposition upon which this study was based, we can conclude that even in the case of the most passive President in modern times, foreign-policy decisions were significantly affected by his style. Specifically, his influence can be discerned in reconciling public opinion to his overall policy position and, given the inevitable institutionalisation of the modern Presidency, in his ability to restrain the policy-making and diplomatic bureaucracies when they appeared to be departing in any essential way from the overall policies he himself had authorised.

Put very simply, in the field of foreign affairs the individual in supreme authority must have the knowledge and prestige to say 'No'. This was an ability that President Truman, who was often overawed by military men, lacked in his handling of General MacArthur. It was an ability that, at least initially, President Kennedy lacked at the time

73

of the Bay of Pigs crisis. It was an ability that often appeared to have been lacking in President Johnson's handling of the Vietnam crisis. In all essential matters it was an ability that President Eisenhower possessed, and which he was not loathe to exercise in the conduct of foreign policy.

Suggestions for further reading

The present work is essentially a study of one aspect of a subject which is increasingly being taught in our universities—namely, foreign policy analysis. There is a rapidly growing literature in this general field. The student who wishes to acquaint himself further with the systematic approach that is seeking to develop theoretical frameworks for analysing foreign policy decision-making will find a broad selection of extracts from books and articles in James Rosenau's *International Politics and Foreign Policy*. The problem with such studies is that they tend to employ a terminology which will be unfamiliar to those who are not well acquainted with the behavioural approach to political science. A work which similarly seeks to provide a conceptual framework for the analysis of foreign policy decision-making, but which employs more comprehensible language, is Joseph Frankel's *The Making of Foreign Policy*.

A fuller list of books about President Eisenhower is given in the general bibliography which follows. Eisenhower's Presidential memoirs, *Mandate for Change* and *Waging Peace*, make dull reading. They are written in a pompous style and, on the whole, are not very revealing. A recent book by Eisenhower, *At Ease*, subtitled, *Stories I Tell to Friends*, reveals more about his early life, but does not deal with his years as President. There are a number of so-called 'campaign biographies'—books written in order to popularise the Presidential candidate—which do reveal something of Eisenhower's background, but obviously in a very partisan manner. Kevin McCann's *Man from Abilene* is possibly the best-known of these. There is, however, some useful background information in a book by Sidney Warren, *The President as World Leader*, which discusses a number of Presidents in respect of their role in international affairs. Marquis Childs' *Eisenhower: Captive Hero*, traces Eisenhower's rise from obscurity to world fame in order to debunk much of the campaign literature described above. Possibly the best book about Eisenhower, however, is Emmet J. Hughes' *The Ordeal of Power*. The author was obviously attracted by Eisenhower and, indeed, became his chief speech-writer, but was disappointed by his performance as President.

The Eisenhower Years, by Richard Rovere, is an excellent collection of articles written by a highly intelligent journalist, and covers all the major events of Eisenhower's Presidency down to 1956. Two works in particular are recommended for their inside accounts of the Eisenhower Presidency. Robert Donovan's *Eisenhower, The Inside Story* is an authoritative account of the Presidency in its first term by a well-known Republican journalist who had access to hitherto unpublished sources of information, including Cabinet Minutes. Sherman Adams' *First-hand Report* is, similarly, an interesting and often revealing account by an essential figure in the Eisenhower Administration.

On contemporary American history, Eric Goldman's *The Crucial Decade—and After* is a racily written, thoroughly absorbing book, which, read in connection with Richard Rovere's book mentioned above, will make much of what has been discussed in the present work in this respect more readily comprehensible.

On the institution of the Presidency, the analyses contained in Clinton Rossiter's *The American Presidency* and in Richard Neustadt's *Presidential Power* are adequate and readily available in cheap paperback editions. For a more detailed, academic approach, E. S. Corwin's *The*

President is a basic work of reference.

On American foreign policy in general one of the best descriptive accounts is John Spanier's *American Foreign Policy since World War II*. For the relationship between strategy and diplomatic policy Seyom Brown's *The Faces of Power* is readable and very up-to-date. W. W. Rostow's *The United States in the World Arena* contains a detailed analysis of American strategic policy, and is especially interesting in that many of its premises can be discerned in the McNamara Doctrine of the Kennedy Administration. Coral Bell's *Negotiation from Strength* contains an excellent analysis of the policies formulated by the United States and Britain in their dealings with the Soviet Union.

Nearly all the books mentioned so far discuss the foreign-policy issues mentioned in this study. However, Herman Finer's *Dulles Over Suez* is a controversial account of the progress of the Suez affair, written as though the reader were actually inside the State Department and the White House. This work is recommended because it contains what purports to be a full account of the roles of the Secretary of State and the President in this crisis.

On John Foster Dulles and his relationship with Eisenhower, Richard Goold-Adams' *The Time of Power* is a more sophisticated biography than the eulogy written by John Robinson Beal, *John Foster Dulles: 1888-1952*.

Finally, on the subject of the relationship between domestic opinion and foreign policy there is Gabriel Almond's often interesting work, *The American People and Foreign Policy*, and there is a very interesting collection of readings in James Rosenau's *Domestic Sources of Foreign Policy*.

Bibliography

ADAMS, S. (1962), *First-Hand Report*, Hutchinson.

BEAL, J. R. (1959), *John-Foster-Dulles: 1888-1959*, Harper, New York.

BELL, C. (1962), *Negotiation from Strength*, Chatto & Windus.

BROWN, S. (1968), *The Faces of Power*, New York: Columbia U.P.

BUTCHER, H. E. (1946), *Three Years with Eisenhower*, Heinemann.

CHILDS, M. (1959), *Eisenhower: Captive Hero*, Hammond, Hammond.

DONOVAN, R. J. (1956), *Eisenhower: The Inside Story*, New York: Harper.

DRUMMOND, R., and COBLENTZ, G. (1961), *Dual at the Brink*, Weidenfeld & Nicolson.

EDEN, A. (1960), *Full Circle*, Cassell.

EISENHOWER, D. D. (1948), *Crusade in Europe*, New York: Doubleday & Co.

— (1963), *Mandate for Change, 1953-1956*, New York: Doubleday & Co.

—(1965), *Waging Peace, 1956-1961*, New York: Doubleday & Co.

— (1968), *At Ease. Stories I Tell to Friends*, Robert Hale.

FINER, H. (1964), *Dulles Over Suez*, Heinemann.

FRANKEL, J. (1963), *The Making of Foreign Policy*, O.U.P.

FREUD, S., and BULLITT, W. C. (1967), *Thomas Woodrow*

Wilson, a Psychological Study, Weidenfeld & Nicolson.

GOLDMAN, E. F. (1962), *The Crucial Decade—and After*, New York: Vintage.

GOOLD-ADAMS, R. (1962), *The Time of Power: The Reappraisal of John Foster Dulles*, Weidenfeld & Nicolson.

HALLE, L. J. (1967), *The Cold War as History*, Chatto & Windus.

HORLICK, A. L., and RUSH, M. (1966), *Strategic Power and Soviet Foreign Policy*, Chicago: Chicago U.P.

HUGHES, E. J. (1963), *The Ordeal of Power. A Political Memoir of the Eisenhower Years*, Macmillan.

IONS, E. (1962), *The Politics of John F. Kennedy*, Routledge & Kegan Paul.

JOHNSON, W. (1963), *1600 Pennsylvania Avenue*, Boston: Little, Brown & Co.

LAFEBER, W. (1967), *America, Russia and The Cold War, 1945-1966*, New York: John Wiley & Sons, Inc.

MCCANN, K. (1952), *Man from Abilene*, Heinemann.

MODELSKI, G. (1962), *A Theory of Foreign Policy*, Pall Mall.

MURPHY, C. J. V., 'The Eisenhower Shift', *Fortune*, January-April 1956.

MURPHY, R. (1964), *Diplomat among the Warriors*, Collins.

NEUSTADT, R. E. (1964), *Presidential Power*, New York: Signet Books.

NIXON, R. M. (1962), *Six Crises*, W. H. Allen.

POLLARD, J. E. (1964), *The Presidents and the Press*, Washington: Public Affairs Press.

Public Papers of the Presidents of the United States, Dwight David Eisenhower, 1953-1961.

PUSEY, M. J. (1956), *Eisenhower The President*, New York: Macmillan.

ROBINSON, J. A., and SNYDER, R. C. 'Decision-Making in International Politics', in KELMAN, H. C. (ed.), *International Behaviour*, pp. 435-63.

ROSENAU, J. N. (ed.) (1961), *International Politics and Foreign Policy*, New York: Free Press of Glencoe Inc.

— (ed.) (1967), *Domestic Sources of Foreign Policy*, New

York: Free Press of Glencoe Inc.

ROSSITER, C. (1960), *The American Presidency*, Rupert Hart-Davies.

ROSTOW, W. W. (1960), *United States in the World Arena*, New York: Harper.

ROVERE, R. H. (1956), *The Eisenhower Years*, New York: Farrar, Straus & Cudahy.

SCHLESINGER, A., Jr. (1965), *A Thousand Days*, Deutsch.

SHANNON, W. V. 'Eisenhower as President', *Commentary*, Vol. 26, No. 5, November 1958, pp. 390-8.

SORENSON, T. C. (1963), *Decision-making in the White House*, New York: Columbia U.P.

— (1965), *Kennedy*, Pan Books.

SPANIER, J. (1965), *American Foreign Policy Since World War II*, New York: Praeger.

TAYLOR, A. (ed.) (1952), *What Eisenhower Thinks*, New York: Thomas Y. Crowell & Co.

WARREN, S. (1964), *The President as World Leader*, New York: J. B. Lippincott Co.